Poverty Knock

a picture of industrial life in the nineteenth century
through songs, ballads and contemporary accounts

selected and edited by
ROY PALMER

CAMBRIDGE UNIVERSITY PRESS

The Resources of Music Series

General Editors: *Wilfrid Mellers, John Paynter*

1. THE RESOURCES OF MUSIC *by Wilfrid Mellers*
2. SOUND AND SILENCE *by John Paynter and Peter Aston*
3. SOMETHING TO PLAY *by Geoffrey Brace*
4. MUSIC DRAMA IN SCHOOLS *edited by Malcolm John*
5. THE PAINFUL PLOUGH *by Roy Palmer*
6. THE VALIANT SAILOR *by Roy Palmer*
7. TROUBADOURS *by Brian Sargent*
8. MINSTRELS *by Brian Sargent*
9. POVERTY KNOCK *by Roy Palmer*

Acknowledgements

Full source references to songs and prose passages are given on pp.62, 63 and 64. Sources of illustrations are listed on p.64. The author and publisher would like to thank all those there listed for permission to reproduce material in this book.

While every effort has been made to contact copyright holders, the publishers apologize if any material has been included without permission.

For valuable assistance in the preparation of the book the author would like to thank the Mitchell Library, Glasgow, Cambridge University Library, Kidderminster Public Library, Sheffield University Library, Manchester Central Library, Aberdeen University Library, Wyn Francis and Katharine Thomson. For guitar chords, Sandra Faulkner. For courtesy, encouragement and support, John Paynter (series editor) and the staff of Cambridge University Press.

Performing and recording rights are reserved and are administered by the Performing Rights Society, The Mechanical Copyright Protection Society and the affiliated bodies throughout the world. Applications should be made to these bodies for a relevant licence. Failure to so apply constitutes a breach of copyright.

The picture on the front cover shows Stockport, about 1850. On the back cover is a watch bearing a slogan used during the campaign for 8-hour days.

Published by the Syndics of the Cambridge University Press
Bentley House, 200 Euston Road, London NW1 2DB
American Branch: 32 East 57th Street, New York, N.Y.10022

© Cambridge University Press 1974

Library of Congress Catalogue Number 73-93391

ISBN 0 521 20443 7

First published 1974

Printed in Great Britain by
Ebenezer Baylis & Son Ltd, Leicester and London

Contents

Epigraph 4   Introduction 5

1 **Factory life: the dreary old drive** 7
   Songs
   1 The jovial cutlers   7
   2 Foster's Mill   9
   3 The factory bell   11
   4 The morn is black   12
   5 The knocker up   13
   6 Poverty knock   14
   7 The doffing mistress   18
   8 The handsome factory girl   19
   9 The merry shoots   20
   10 The carpet weavers' true tale 21
   11 The Preston steam-loom weaver 22
   12 The Coventry weaver   24
   13 Nailers' song   26
   14 The nailmakers' strike   27
   15 The poor nailmaker   29
   16 Tally i o, the grinder!   30
   17 Joe, the factory lad   34
   18 The matchgirls' song   35
   19 Holly ho   36

2 **Pit life: down among the coal** 38
   Songs
   20 Down the pit we want to go   39
   21 Working today   39
   22 The pony driver   41
   23 The collier lass   44
   24 The collier   46
   25 Five in the morning   48
   26 The collier lads   50
   27 Down among the coal   52
   28 Lament for John Sneddon   53
   29 The Gresford disaster   56
   30 The brave Dudley boys   58
   31 O bury the blackleg   59
   32 The collier lad's lament   60

Suggestions for further activities   62
Sources   62
Index of song titles and first lines   64

Epigraph

I remember there was two men killed at the Birtley New Pit. And I'll never forget the indignity of those men being brought home. They picked them up, put them in a sack and trundled them to their home in a hand-cart. I know this man – they called him Fawcett – and he'd left seven or eight bairns. And I was only tiny but I remembered this hand-cart coming up, and these two bundles, you know, and coarse sacking on the thing. (Em Elliott of Birtley, Co. Durham, 1961)

Every morning at five a clock the Warden is to ring a bell for beginning to work, at eight a clock for breakfast, at half an hour after for work again, at twelve a clock for dinner, at one to work and at eight to ring for leaving work and all to be lock'd up. (Law Book of the Crowley Iron Works, 1700)

The apprentices slept about fifty in a room. The governor used to unlock the door of each room when the first bell rang; having unlocked the last room door, he went back to the first with a switch stick in his hand, and if he found anyone in bed, or slowly dressing, he used to lay on without mercy; by which severity, the rooms were soon empty. The apprentices had their breakfast generally of water-porridge, called in this part of Derbyshire 'stir-pudding', and oaten cake, which they took in the mill. The breakfast hour was eight o'clock; but the machinery did not stop, and so irregular were their meals, it sometimes did not arrive till ten or eleven o'clock. At other times the overlookers would not allow the apprentices to eat it, and it stood till it grew cold and covered with flue. Forty minutes were allowed for dinner; of which time, full one half was absorbed in cleaning the frames. Sometimes the overlookers denied them in the mill the whole dinner-time, on which occasion a half-penny was given, or rather promised. On these occasions, they had to work the whole day through, generally sixteen hours, without food or rest. (*A memoir of Robert Blincoe*, 1832)

Introduction

Primitive work processes were often accompanied by singing. Spinning and weaving, for example, or soothing a baby to sleep, or milking a cow, had songs with rhythms appropriate to the activity concerned. Apart from such individual tasks, team work was often accompanied by song. The sea shanties of the last century are group work songs, as are the chants of the Hebridean cloth fullers and the Portland quarrymen, which survived until very recent years.

In addition to work songs, people frequently made songs about work. These might be descriptions of various crafts and trades, sometimes highly romanticised, and often full of jaunty good humour. They might be sung in leisure time, but also in the workshop itself, before the advent of heavy machinery. In light industries, the practice of singing at work continued until this century, until it was replaced by 'Music while you work' or Radio 1. The heavy or noisy machinery which came in with the industrial revolution removed the need for work songs and usually obliterated any other singing – except that of power loom weavers who often communicated by means of lip-reading. William Holt, an old weaver of Todmorden, remembered the weavers singing hymns, songs and snatches from the *Messiah*, partly by lip-reading, and partly because 'It was just possible to hear the high notes above the roar of the machinery' (*I haven't unpacked*).

For many years, it was thought that this was the end of the story, that industry and the towns combined to smother folk song within a generation. Happily, songs continued to be made and sung in the industrial communities. The miners continued their longstanding tradition of song in many areas of England: the North-east, Yorkshire and Lancashire, the Midlands, and South Wales are all represented in this book. In many ways, miners' songs resemble those of the sailors, whose contest with wind and water is paralleled by that of the miners with another element, the earth; a shipwreck has similarities with a pit disaster, sea battles might be compared with strikes and lock-outs in industry, while bitter complaints about pay and conditions are common to both spheres. The sailor was at once despised as a good-for-nothing and admired as a hero; so was the miner.

Textile workers are another group which was established long before the industrial revolution, and thus had the strength to cling to some of its traditions afterwards. Weavers and spinners from Lancashire and Yorkshire, Belfast doffers, Nottingham lace makers, Coventry ribbon weavers, and Kidderminster carpet weavers are all represented here.

Some industries have little to offer by way of songs. The heavy iron and steel industry, for example, seems to have produced nothing. The lighter parts of this industry, however, are illustrated by songs of Sheffield cutlers and grinders, and of Black Country nail and chainmakers.

Running through all these songs there are common subjects and themes. Pay and conditions, poverty, danger, struggle: these are the main preoccupations. They are lightened from time to time by humour, by courage, by humanity. The earliest songs included date from the 1780s and 90s. From this period until the early 1840s, the singers often look back towards a better time which went before. There is then a change of perspective, and singers begin to look forward to a better future, wrested if necessary from a reluctant society. The factor common to both situations is a distaste for the time in which the singer was actually present. The debate about the benefits (or otherwise) conferred by the industrial revolution still goes on among historians but people who were present at the time seem to have been on the side of the pessimists.

Pessimistic or not, they continued to make songs. The latest in this book, *The Gresford disaster*, dates from 1934. It is by no means the last of its kind, but part of a continuing tradition. Such songs, like their pre-industrial cousins, celebrated the skill and strength of the workpeople and chronicled their lives and labours. They were a means of communication and of propaganda. Often, in printed form, they had the practical purpose of raising money for strikers or the unemployed.

The songs are juxtaposed with prose passages. The chief source which has been used for factories is William Dodd, a man who was himself crippled by his work. In the early 1840s he travelled round the country and wrote a series of letters to Lord Shaftesbury on the evils of the factory system, which were later published. Shaftesbury used some of this material in the campaign which led to the passing of the Factory Act of 1844, which limited the hours of work for women to twelve a day and provided safety regulations for dangerous machinery. (Attempts were later made to discredit some of Dodd's work; the evidence from the songs would appear to support him.)

The main source used here for nineteenth-century mining is Thomas Burt, a Durham pitman, born in 1837, who later became a Liberal M.P. and Privy Councillor. In many cases, however, the recollections of living people have been used. Some of Walter Haydn Davies' memories have been included from his splendid book, *The right place, the right time*, and I have also transcribed tape recordings of interviews with a number of ordinary people, or printed their letters.

The great strength of this material, both songs and prose, is that it reflects the views of those who were undergoing the experiences of which they write or which they recreate in an idiom which they felt to be their own. We are dealing with historical documents of considerable interest, but over and above this, we are receiving a wave of communication from the past, which conveys in very human terms the feelings and the hopes and the struggles of men and women at work.

Currency

Sums of money mentioned in the text are in terms of pounds, shillings and pence, and I therefore give below a brief table of decimal equivalents. It is difficult to make comparisons between the different values of money at different times, without reference to average earnings, or the ways in which people tend to spend those earnings. John Burnett's *History of the cost of living* (Penguin, 1969) provides very useful information on all these matters.

£	s	d		£ p
		6	=	2½
	1	0	=	5
	2	6	=	12½
	10	0	=	50
1	0	0	=	1·00

12 pence (old) = one shilling
20 shillings = one pound
1 guinea = 21 shillings

Sir Thomas Lombe's silk factory, Derby, built 1733

1

Factory life: the dreary old drive

Song 1 *The jovial cutlers*

Bro-ther work-men, cease your la-bour, Lay your files and ham-mers by; Lis-ten while a

bro-ther neigh-bour Sings a cut-ler's des-tin-y: How up-on a good Saint Mon-day,

Sit-ting by the smith-y fire, Tell-ing what's been done o't Sun-day, And in cheer-ful mirth con-spire.

2 Soon I hear the trap-door rise up:
On the ladder stands my wife:
'Damn thee, Jack, I'll dust thy eyes up,
Thou leads a plaguy, drunken life;
Here thou sits instead of working,
Wi' thy pitcher on thy knee.
Curse thee, thou'd be always lurking,
And I may slave myself for thee.

3 'Ah, thou great fat, idle devil,
Now I see thy goings on;
Here thou sits all't day to revel,
Ne'er a stroke o' work thou's done;
See thee, look what stays I've gotten,
See thee, what a pair of shoes;
Gown and petticoat half rotten,
Ne'er a whole stitch in my hose.

4 'Pray thee, look here, all the forenoon,
Thou hast wasted with thy idle way;
When does t'a mean to get thy sours done,
Thy mester wants 'em in today?
Thou knows, I hate to broil and quarrel,
But I've neither soap nor tea;
'Od burn thee, Jack, forsake thy barrel,
Or never more thou'st lie with me.'

5 Now once more on joys be thinking,
Since hard scolding's tired my wife;
The course is clear, let's have some drink in,
And toast a jovial cutler's life.
For her foul tongue, fie upon her,
Shall we our pleasures thus give o'er?
No, we'll good Saint Monday honour,
When brawling wives shall be no more.

There is a tradition that this song was written in 1780 or 1790 by an old cutler nick-named 'Bone-heft', after the bone-handled knives that he made. It gives a picture of the pre-industrial workshop, with its less hectic pace, its smaller scale, and its greater flexibility with regard to time. Saint Monday was the custom of taking Monday off. This meant, of course, that the workmen had to work much harder for the rest of the week, in order to catch up; but at least they enjoyed the additional leisure beforehand. Saint Monday was vigorously opposed by employers during the nineteenth century. 'Sours' are articles paid for in advance but not yet done.

Sheffield smithies

'Smithy', in Sheffield, is becoming an obsolete term; instead of speaking of 'ahr smithy', our cutlery makers have 'my factory', or 'warehouse', or 'workshops'. To realise the old Sheffield smithy you must picture to yourself a stone building, of similar workmanship to common field walls, seven or eight yards long by four wide, and seven feet high to the rise of the roof. It is open to the slates or thatch. The door is in the middle of one side, with the fireplace facing it; and at either end is a hearth, with the bellows in the corner, and the 'stithy stocks' in their proper situations. The walls are plastered over with clay or 'wheel swarf', to keep the wind out of the crevices; sometimes the luxury of a rough coat of lime may even be indulged in. The floor is of mud, the windows, about half a yard wide and a yard long, have white paper, well saturated in boiled oil, instead of glass, or in summer are open to the air. In one corner is a place partitioned off 'for t'mester' as a warehouse or store room, and on each side are the work-boards with vices for hafters, putters together, etc. Over the fireplace is a paddywhack almanack, and the walls are covered with last dying speeches and confessions, *Death and the Lady*, wilful murders, Christmas carols, lists of all the running horses, and so forth. Hens use the smithy for their roosting place, and some times other live stock have a harbour there – as rabbits, guinea pigs, or ducks, while the walls are not destitute of singing birds' cages. There are odorous out-offices close adjoining, and it is essential that the whole should be within easy call from the back door of 't'mester's house'. (R. E. Leader, *Reminiscences of old Sheffield*, 1876.)

The cutler, 1825

Song 2 *Foster's Mill*

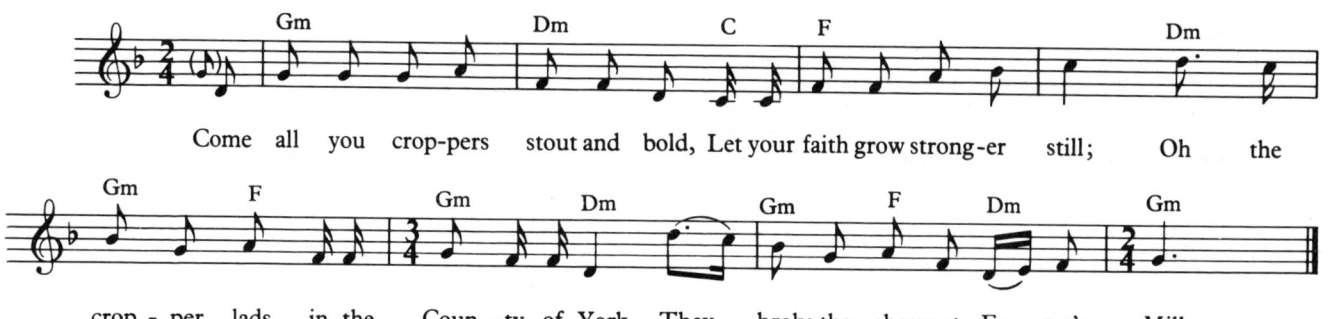

Come all you crop-pers stout and bold, Let your faith grow strong-er still; Oh the crop-per lads in the Coun-ty of York, They broke the shears at Fos-ter's Mill.

2 The wind it blew, the sparks they flew,
   Which alarmed the town full soon;
   And out of bed poor people did creep
   And run by the light of the moon.

3 Around and around they all did stand
   And solemnly did swear:
   Neither bucket nor kit, nor any such thing,
   Should be of assistance there.

4 Around and around we all will stand
   And sternly swear we will:
   We'll break the shears and windows too,
   And set fire to the tazzling mill.

The last verse may be used as a chorus.

Foster's Mill: this mill stood between Horbury and Ossett (near Wakefield) in Yorkshire. The attack on it took place on 9 April 1812, when a crowd of between three and six hundred, armed with firearms, hatchets and clubs, destroyed gig mills, shear frames and cloth, together with a number of windows, the total damage being estimated at £700. The gig mills were machines for raising the nap on cloth by hand, and the shear frames semi-mechanised the trimming of the nap. Both practices were opposed by the workpeople, especially the croppers or shear men, who were the main force behind the Luddite movement in Yorkshire. A tazzling mill is a gig mill.

The croppers were well-paid workmen who were quickly reduced to penury by the introduction of mechanisation to their craft. It has been estimated that between 1806 and 1817 the number of shears operated by machinery in Yorkshire increased from 100 to 1462. By the latter date, of the remaining 3378 croppers, 1170 were unemployed and 1445 partly so.

'The introduction of machinery is the chief cause of their misery'

I have this day been in various directions about the town, and I have seen much misery. In the morning I met about twenty men sweeping the streets, and on inquiry found they were mostly men who had served a legal time to some trade, such as croppers, flax-dressers, and others connected with the manufactures. They generally affirm that the introduction of machinery is the chief cause of their misery; they are employed by the parish at 1s per day, and in consequence of the great number of applications, they are only allowed to work two and three days a-week, as the case may require.

From them I went to the outside of the town, near Water-lane, where I saw a number of men breaking stones for the roads, and others standing with their hands in their pockets looking on. I was very much surprised to see the immense quantity of stones these men had broken...They are generally men who have been thrown out of employment by the introduction of machinery, according to their own account, and are now employed, like those sweeping streets, at 1s a day.

These men say that when they were employed in their own work, they could earn from 5s to 7s per day, and could then maintain their families in comfort; but now they are under the necessity of sending their wives and children to the factories, to assist in supporting them.

I have also had an interview with some woollen-cloth-dressers, commonly called croppers; these men were formerly in the habit of earning from 36s to 40s per week by hand, and were obliged to serve a term of five or seven years to the trade. In 1814, there were 1733 croppers in Leeds, all in full employment; and now, since the introduction of machinery, the whole of the cloth manufactured in this town is dressed by a comparatively small number, chiefly boys, at from 5s to 8s..., and a few men at from 10s to 14s per week. The old croppers have turned themselves to any thing they can get to do; some acting as bailiffs, water-carriers, scavengers, or selling oranges, cakes, tapes and laces, gingerbread, blacking, &c. &c. (William Dodd, writing from Leeds on 28 September 1841.)

If we look at the condition of the croppers, flax-dressers, wool-combers, hand-loom weavers, calico printers, &c., previously to the introduction of machinery, we shall find that all these were flourishing trades, the earnings varying from £1 to £2 per week; that the husband could then support his family by his own unassisted industry; and that he was not then required to rise in the morning at the sound of the bell; but was comparatively an independent man. As machinery became more general, the wages, as a matter of course, became less, in consequence of a number of hands having been thrown out of employment. The husband then finding that his earnings were insufficient to meet the family expenses, was under the necessity of sending first the children, then his wife, to work in the factories; those places which had monopolised his trade and calling. These women and children being made, with the assistance of machinery, to do the work of men, the men were cast off, or reduced in point of wages to a level with the women. We now find that men in the above trades are working, for from 6s to 10s per week, longer hours than they were working a few years ago for four times the amount. (William Dodd, 18 January 1842.)

Croppers at John Wood's workshop near Huddersfield

Song 3 *The factory bell*

    2 You've just got time to eat and sleep:
       A man is set your time to keep;
       And if you chance to come too late,
       You're marked on paper or on slate.
       No matter e'er what be the cause,
       You must abide by their own laws;
       And at the time you draw your wage
       For coming late there's so much charged.

    3 Some wheedling foreman every hour
       Makes big himself with stolen power;
       He hectoring goes in every place:
       Few know his heart who see his face.
       But masters, they are not to blame:
       The men are worst, you know the same;
       For man to make himself a king
       Cares not who sink if he but swim.

    4 Oh haste on wings of flight that day
       When man to man shall kindly say:
       We all forget, we all forgive,
       We all in golden days shall live.
       Now wouldn't it be a pleasing sight
       For man to man to do what's right?
       Each would enjoy his little store
       And die in peace when life is o'er.

* This is a C chord with an A added by stopping the G string on the second fret.

Factory workers for many generations were summoned to work by a bell. The factory hooter or bull is a relatively late development.

Song 4 *The morn is black*

The morn is black as a raven, the streets are wet and cold; The mill is mournfully telling it's time that I should go. Another day at the loom, my lass, where shuttles they do fly;* The noise is like to screaming when some they come to die.

* See Song 6, Verse 6

2 Oh the whistle is a-blowing, sleep my bonny bairn;
Oh the whistle is a-blowing, it's time for me to go.
Oh the wheels they go a-turning and the noise it makes thee scream;
There's a racing and a going and the hissing of the steam.

'Up every morning at five'

In 1730, at the age of 7, William Hutton started his apprenticeship at a Derby silk-mill. 'I had now to rise at five every morning during seven years', he wrote, 'submit to the cane whenever convenient for the master, be the constant companion of the most rude and vulgar of the human race.' An incident in the following year underlines his anxiety over arriving on time: Christmas holidays were attended with snow, followed by a sharp frost. A thaw came on, in the afternoon of the 27th, but in the night the ground was again caught by a frost, which glazed the streets. 'I did not awake, the next morning, till daylight seemed to appear. I rose in tears, for fear of punishment, and went to my father's bedside, to ask what was o'clock? "He believed six". I darted out in agonies, and, from the bottom of Full street, to the top of Silk-mill lane, not 200 yards, I fell nine times! Observing no lights in the mill, I knew it was an early hour, and that the reflection of the snow had deceived me. Returning, it struck two. As I now went with care, I fell but twice.' (William Hutton, *Life*, 1816.)

Michael Hopkins lives in Galloway's-yard, West-street. He was born at Skircoat, near Halifax. His mother was left a widow, with a family of thirteen children; and their united earnings procured them food. He was sent to the mill of Henry Lodge, Esq., at Lower Willow-hall, near Halifax, at the age of six years, and received no wages for twelve months, excepting a penny or two occasionally, as the overlooker thought fit. At the age of seven, he had 1s 6d weekly, with an advance of 2½d per week yearly for the succeeding period. At the age of fourteen years, he had 3s per week. He commenced work before five o'clock in the morning, and continued at work till eight o'clock at night, without stopping for breakfast or drinking (tea), and had only three-quarters of an hour for dinner! If more, it was always worked up at night! And, during the whole time of working hours, they were never allowed to sit, even for five minutes, without receiving a kick, or a blow, or such like! (William Dodd, writing from Leeds on 27 September 1841.)

Work in cotton factories

The operatives in cotton factories begin to work at half-past five, or six in the morning, and cease at half-past seven, or eight at night. The work of spinners and stretchers is among the most laborious that exist, and is exceeded, perhaps, by that of mowing alone; and few mowers, we believe, think of continuing their labour for twelve hours without intermission...

The labour of the other classes of hands employed in factories, as carders, rovers, piecers, and weavers, consists not so much in their actual manual exertion, which is very moderate, as in the constant attention which they are required to keep up, and the intolerable fatigue of standing for so great a length of time. (William Dodd, quoting a manufacturer, in a letter from Bury, 28 October 1841.)

Song 5 *The knocker up*

A pal of mine once said to me, 'Will you knock me up at half past three?' And so, promptly at

half past one, I knocked him up and said, 'Oh, John, I've just come round to tell you,

I've just come round to tell you, I've just come round to tell you, You've got two more hours to sleep'.

Knocker up: a person who went round to wake up workpeople, sometimes by tapping on their bedroom windows with a long stick; known in the North-east as a 'caller'. Exact time-keeping ('Time is money') was one of the features of the industrial revolution which people found hardest to accept.

Cotton factories, Union Street, Manchester, 1835

Song 6 Poverty knock

2 Oh dear, we're goin' to be late;
  Gaffer is stood at the gate.
  We're out o' pocket, our wages they're dockit,
  We'll 'a' to buy grub on the slate.

3 And when our wages they'll bring,
  We're often short of a string;
  And while we are fratchin' wi' gaffer for snatchin',
  We know to his brass he will cling.

4 We've got to wet our own yarn
  By dippin' it into the tarn;
  It's wet and soggy and makes us feel groggy,
  And there's mice in that dirty old barn.

5 Oh dear, my poor 'ead it sings;
  I should have woven three strings,
  But threads are breakin' and my back is achin',
  Oh dear, I wish I had wings.

6 Sometimes a shuttle flies out
  And gives some poor woman a clout.
  There she lies bleedin', but nobody's 'eedin';
  Who's goin' to carry her out?

7   Tuner should tackle my loom:
    'E'd rather sit on his bum.
    'E's far too busy a-courtin' our Lizzie,
    And I cannot get 'im to come.

8   Lizzie's so easy led,
    I think that 'e takes her to bed.
    She always was skinny, now look at her pinny,
    I think it's high time they was wed.

Guttle: eat. A string: length of cloth. Fratchin': quarreling. A shuttle flies out: 'It appears there are a great number of accidents in this neighbourhood, some very serious ones; the eyes seem to be in great danger from the shuttle flying out in the act of weaving in power-looms'. (William Dodd, writing from Ashton-under-Lyne, 20 November 1841.) Tuner: maintenance man.

The advent of power loom weaving forced down the wages of the hand-loom weavers, who became known as 'poverty knockers'. After the early 1830s conditions became even worse for the hand-loom weavers, though, for that matter, life was by no means good in the mills. The old Dobbie loom seemed to make the sound of 'poverty knock' as it worked, hence the refrain of this song. Most of the early factory weavers were women and boys, and this song has always struck me as being a woman's words. This version, however, was sung by an old Batley weaver, Tom Daniel, who first heard it in the early 1900s.

Spinning cotton yarns in a Lancashire mill, 1897

Lace making

A factory girl's day

In selecting a situation for my place of residence, during my temporary stay in Manchester, I was actuated by a desire to be as much as possible among the working classes; accordingly, I took lodgings in the vicinity of some factories...The daughter of the people with whom I lodge is working in one of these factories...Previously to retiring on the first night, I was told that I should hear a knocking at the window in the morning, and was not to be alarmed, as it was only for the purpose of calling their daughter up to work...

At about half past four o'clock (mark the time), a rattling noise was heard at the window...The watchman, or person who performs this duty (for which he gets 3d per head, per week, from all he calls up in the mornings), then went to the next house, and so on through the streets, disturbing the whole neighbourhood, till the noise of his 'infernal machine' died away in the distance. This machine...is somewhat similar to a shepherd's crook, only longer in the handle, to enable the person using it to reach the upper windows...

The watchful, waking mother, well knowing the consequence of being too late, is now heard at the bedside of her daughter, rousing the unwilling girl to another day of toil. At length you hear her on the floor; the clock is striking five. Then for the first time, the girl becomes conscious of the necessity for haste; and having slipped on her clothes, and (if she thinks there is time) washed herself, she takes a drink of cold coffee, which has been left standing in the fireplace, a mouthful of bread (if she can eat it), and having packed up her breakfast in her handkerchief, hastens to the factory. The bell rings as she leaves the threshold of her home. Five minutes more, and she is in the factory, stripped and ready for work. The clock strikes half-past five; the engine starts, and her day's work commences.

At half-past seven, and in some factories at eight, the engine slacks its pace (seldom stopping) for a short time, till the hands have cleared the machinery, and swallowed a little food. It then goes on again, and continues at full speed till twelve o'clock, when it stops for dinner. Previously to leaving the factory, and in her dinner hour, she has her machines to clean. The distance of the factory is about five minutes' walk from her home. I noticed every day that she came in at half-past twelve, or within a minute or two, and once she was over the half hour; the first thing she did was to wash herself, then get her dinner (which she was seldom able to eat), and pack up her drinking for the afternoon. This done, it was time to be on her way to work again, where she remains, without one minute's relaxation, till seven o'clock; she then comes home, and throws herself into a chair exhausted. This repeated *six* days in a week (save that on Saturdays she may get back a little earlier, say, an hour or two), can there be any wonder at their preferring to lie in bed until dinner-time, instead of going to church on the *seventh*? (William Dodd, writing from Manchester, 16 October 1841.)

Factory mothers

I find there are a great many women employed in winding and reeling, and in power-loom weaving, in these cotton factories; working, in every respect, under the same distressing circumstances as the generality of factory labourers. I was very much hurt to see the mothers in a morning, at the first sound of the factory bell, running with their infants in their arms, wrapped in a piece of old blanket or rug, to the house of the person who is to take charge of them for the day; and then hurrying off to the factory, in order to get in before the gates were closed, as they know very well that if they are half a minute too late, a fine of 2d or 3d will be entered against them: which fine it will take them as many hours' work to redeem, and often more. (William Dodd, writing from Bolton, 8 October 1841.)

Fines in factories

Fines are levied on various occasions. I have seen, early in the morning, at Stockport and other places, from fifty to a hundred men, women, and children, standing at the door of a factory, locked out for being half a minute too late. And, on making enquiry, I found they would all be fined, the men 3d, the women 2d, and the children 1d, and that it would take from ten or eleven o'clock in the forenoon to earn their fines. The above scale of fines for being late is moderate. At some places the men are fined 6d; and at many places 4d; many of these masters being in the constant habit of robbing the children and young people without the slightest scruple of a part of the meal-times which the Legislature has endeavoured to secure them. Now, let us see, my Lord, how this system of fines will affect the master. The hands generally work by piece, so that their being out a few minutes longer is very little injury to him; and by keeping, say, ten of each, men, women, and children, a few minutes at the gate twice a day, he would realise a profit of £3 per week from this source alone; but I have reason to believe it is much greater in many factories.

Another source of profit to the manufacturers, in connexion with fines, arises from alleged bad work in spinning, weaving, &c. In the spinning department the overlooker goes round and examines the cops as they are taken from the spindles, and writes on a slip of paper his opinion (of course he has his instructions); for instance, he will write 'good yarn, but soft cops', or 'fair cops, but indifferent yarn'. This slip of paper is fastened to a cop on the top of the pile for the inspection of the master, who calls out on seeing it, – 'How is this? why don't you make better cops?' and, without waiting for a reply, continues 'I shall fine you 6d', which is accordingly booked against the spinner. I have conversed with some men whose fines amounted in all to 6s, and upwards, in a week; and a great number whose fines were 3s to 4s per week. In the weaving department, they generally throw the piece, however slightly injured, upon the weaver's hands, taking care to charge 1s to 1s 6d more for it than the market. The poor weaver has to lose considerably by selling it at an under rate, or exchanging it for other goods. (William Dodd, 18 January 1842.)

Power loom weaving

I was very much surprised with the great room here for power-loom weaving, which is, perhaps, the largest in Lancashire; containing 1,058 power-looms all busily at work, excepting a few which were undergoing repairs. These looms give employment to 521 weavers, chiefly young men and women; 22 overlookers, 18 twisters, 6 winders, 2 drawers, and 2 heald-pickers; in all 571 persons. They are now working only 8 hours per day. These 1,058 power-looms are capable of weaving, when working full-time, 3,900 cuts per week, each averaging 46 yards long, 36 inches wide, and 52 picks of weft to the inch. They are weaving, generally, strong cotton shirtings, sheetings, &c. I was taken through a store-room nearly filled with these goods, standing pile upon pile, over a great extent of ground; and to a question I asked as to the number, I was told that there were nearly 300,000 pieces, all ready for the market. (William Dodd, writing about Fielden's factory at Todmorden, 1 November 1841.)

Ackroyd's loom shed at Halifax in the 1840s

Song 7 *The doffing mistress*

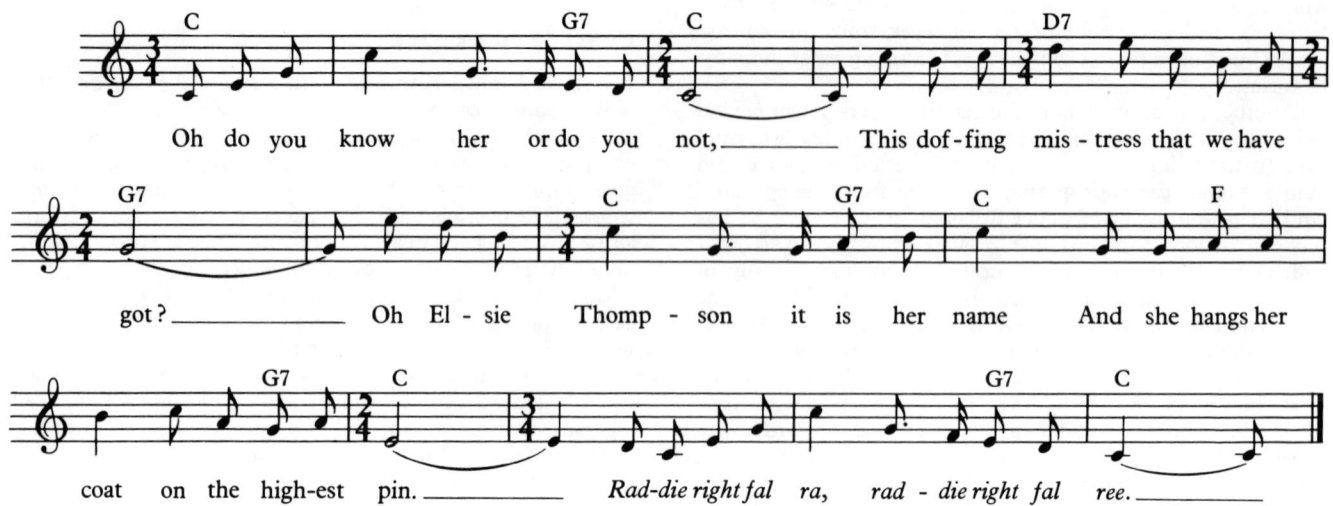

2 On Monday morning when she comes in,
   She hangs her coat on the highest pin;
   She turns around just to greet her friends,
   Saying, all you weavers, tie up your ends.

3 Tie up our ends, we will surely do;
   Our hands are steady, our hearts are true.
   Tie up our ends, we will surely do,
   But for Lizzie Murphy and not for you.

4 Oh Lizzie Murphy are you going away;
   Is it tomorrow, or is it today?
   Your going away, it'll break our hearts;
   There'll be no one left now to take our part.

Doffing: work of placing empty bobbins on the spinning machines and removing full ones. The women so engaged were (and are) called doffers. Mistress: fore-woman.

This song has been called the national anthem of the Belfast textile mills, where it is still sung. Many doffers were crook-backed from their work of carrying heavy bobbins, which gives an ironic twist to the line, 'She hangs her coat on the highest pin'.

Song 8   *The handsome factory girl*

All you that love a bit of fun, give ear to what I say, And you shall have a quart of ale upon my wedding day; For I'll call for liquor merrily and cut a noble swell, And matrimony I will read all with the fact'ry girl.

2   The factory lass I do adore and shall for evermore:
     It would revive a nobleman to see her curl her hair.
     Her temper's made of harmony, she'd charm you with her spell,
     And there's no one so enticing as the handsome factory girl.

3   So always use them tenderly when you are so inclined,
     And they will please you to the heart according to your mind;
     But should you prove obstreperous and make their bellies swell,
     Then weekly wages you must pay unto the factory girl.

4   If you attempt to run away, or cannot pay the brass,
     The maidens they will beat you as neat as you can cast;
     And the overseer will send you unto the treading mill,
     And make you pay, or else consent to wed the factory girl.

5   May God send us a healthy spring, likewise a flourishing trade,
     That a workman he can spend a crown and never be afraid.
     Here's success to every spinner lad that in the world does dwell,
     And I'll live my life for evermore with the handsome factory girl.

Weekly wages: an allowance. Brass: money. Treading mill: treadmill (a form of punishment, in prison). Crown: 5*s.*

Song 9 *The merry shoots*

2   The bobbin and the carriage hands they scarcely would look down
    Or bend their portly bodies for to pick up half a crown;
    And if it had but lasted long, I think they wouldn't stoop
    To poor beef steaks and onions, but they'd dine on turtle soup.

3   The cobbler left his soles and heels and wouldn't be so mean
    As stick to wax and tatching ends, but bought a twist machine;
    The tailor left his board and goose, the miller left his grist;
    Tag rag and bobtail all got loose to get into the twist.

4   And servants left the mop and broom and wouldn't go to place,
    But set their dainty hands to work to purl and mend the lace;
    But to tell the long and short of it, and so to end my song,
    Amongst so many twisters, sir, they've twisted it too strong.

Tatching ends: cobbler's thread. Goose: pressing iron.

During the years 1823 to 1825 there was a boom in the lace industry in Nottingham, because of the lapse of patent restrictions on the trade. The collapse of the market, in 1826, gave rise to this song.

Unemployment

In examining the Manchester list of prices for mule-spinning, I find the same premium held out to the manufacturers as at Bolton and elsewhere, to enlarge their wheels, and do with fewer hands; and this will account for the many cotton spinners I have met with out of employment. In 1836, there were upwards of 2,000 cotton spinners in full work in Manchester; in 1841, there were only 600 employed. Knowing this, I was not surprised to see scores walking about the streets with nothing to do; others employed in going errands, waiting upon the market people, selling pins and needles, ballads, tapes and laces, oranges, gingerbread, &c. &c.; while those who are in work are killing themselves by over-exertion. (William Dodd, writing from Manchester, 16 October 1841.)

Song 10 *The carpet weavers' true tale*

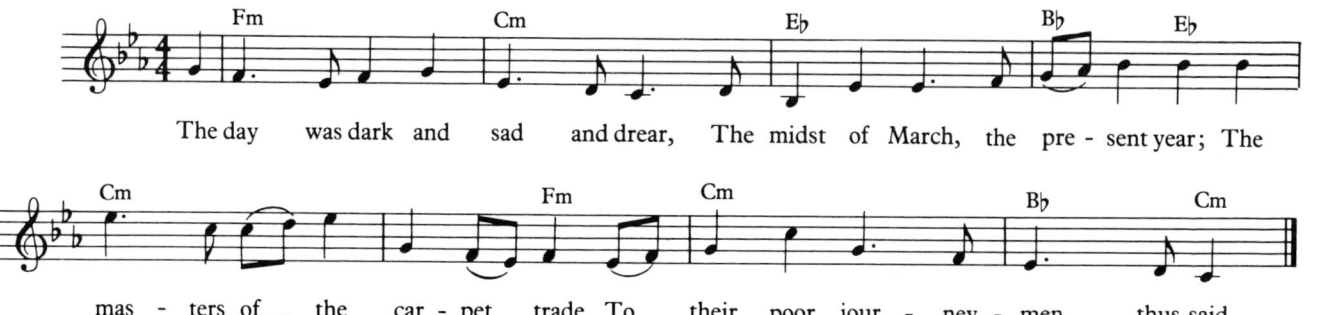

2 'In the *Evening Mail* we do declare
That you both drunk and idle are;
Therefore we have resolved and say
We'll have more work and give less pay.

3 'It takes us now full twenty years
Of close attention, anxious cares,
To gain a fortune which, in ten,
We'll get by grinding journeymen.

4 'Potatoes, oatmeal, you must eat,
Nor dare to think of butcher's meat' –
While they to noblemen aspire
In equipage and rich attire.

5 So Pharoah to God's Israel said:
'You're idle, idle; earn your bread'.
So Greece and Rome, we find, did have
In ancient times, their lords and slaves.

6 Their business now is at a stand,
And we will go throughout the land;
The masters made a great mistake:
We'll die before their pride we'll take.

7 Give to our families in distress,
Left for a season fatherless;
Your kind relief, a pittance give
And you our best thanks shall receive.

Carpets are still made at Kidderminster, in Worcestershire. The past history of the industry was often turbulent. There was a strike in 1828, when 'practically the whole trade of the town was brought to a standstill by the carpet-weavers' six months resistance to a reduction of 17% in their wages' (S. and B. Webb, *History of trade unionism*, 1902, p.98). The population of the town at the time was between 12 and 14,000, of whom some 4000 were engaged in making carpets. The payment for a yard of carpet was usually 1*s*, a price which had been standard since 1816. A weaver could earn about 15*s* a week, out of which he would have to pay a boy to assist him. The employers argued that reductions in prices were needed to meet competition in the North of England and Scotland. They also said that technical improvements had made the work easier, and that the workers earned too much, and spent their money on drink. The weavers were prepared to take a cut, but not of 2*d* in the shilling. To the masters' talk of sacrifices, they replied: 'Judging from appearances, we are not aware that *you* had made *any* sacrifices. It is obvious that for many years you have realised large profits. Ought not the reduction to have been made from the amount of those profits; and not from the wages of the workmen?'

A bitter strike ensued, which lasted from March until August. During it, there was a considerable propaganda battle, conducted by handbills, placards and home-made ballads. Three of these have survived, of which our song is one. Apart from their propaganda value, the ballads were sold in and around Kidderminster in order to provide a little income for the strikers.

Song 11 *The Preston steam-loom weaver*

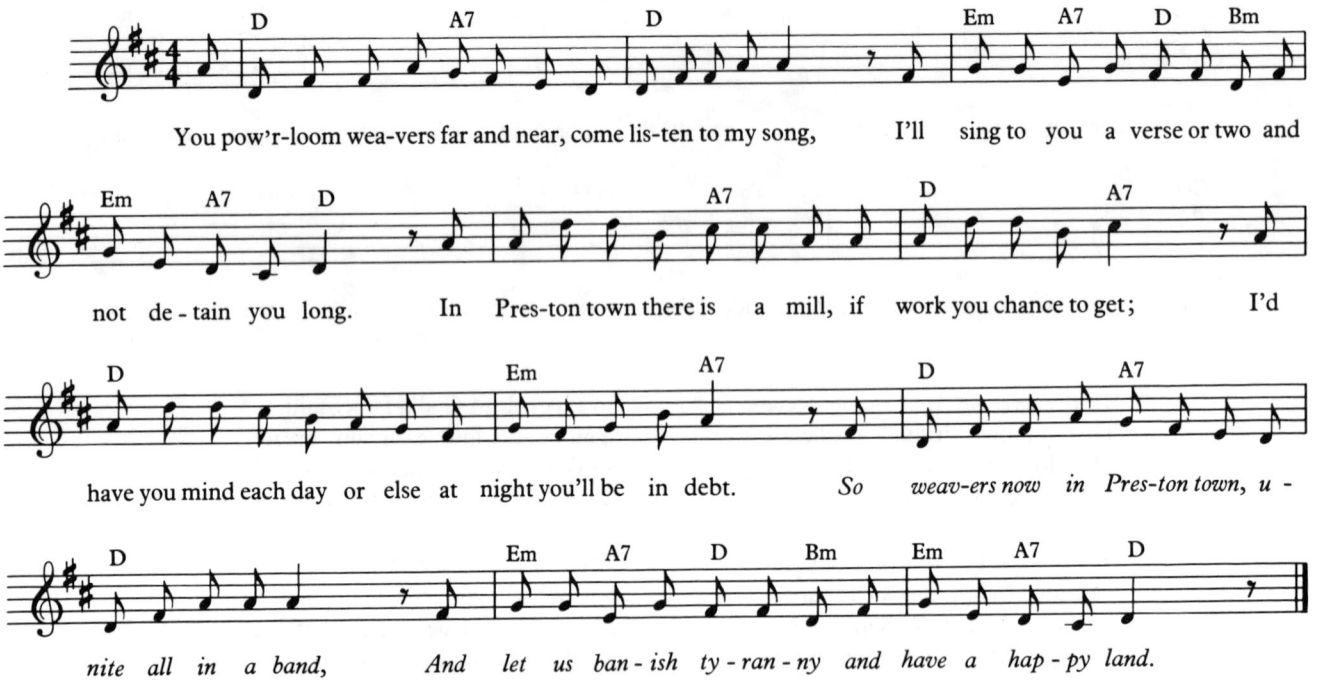

2. In the morning just at six o'clock the engine does begin;
   You must set off a-running, for a prize you have to win,
   For should it happen that you be ten minutes there too late,
   You must give in your number and twopence they will bate.

3. And while the engine's running, oh, I'm sure it's very hard:
   There's threepence more if you should chance to go out in the yard.
   If anything about your looms should chance to break that day,
   There's no excuse, they'll tell you plain, you will get off for pay.

4. Four shillings for a temple box and eight pence for a stud,
   Six or eightpence for a fork, they'll suck your very blood;
   Two shillings for a driving wheel, two pence for one day's waste,
   Three pence for a gold bobbin if it does not run its race.

5. Should sickness overtake you and you stay away one day,
   Two shillings they will fine you, or else they'll stop your pay;
   And should you never mend again, it's true what I have said,
   You must go and serve your notice out, boys, after you are dead.

6. The engineers of England are doing all they can
   And standing up in every town to help their fellowman.
   Then Preston weavers do the same and stand firm every one,
   And other towns will back you up, assist you all they can.

7. Now to conclude and make an end, let's all unite, and quick,
   And never cease to labour till we drive *him* to old Nick;
   For these have always been his plans, both town and country knows;
   The devil his rights will never have till he's got him in his claws.

The Preston strike and lock-out

Preston has become somewhat celebrated as the principal 'battle field', where the capital and labour engaged in the cotton manufacture fight in defence of what each deems its respective rights or privileges. As a manufacturing town, Preston possesses a few advantages, combined with some drawbacks. It is thirty miles from the chief market at Manchester, and some distance north of the great Lancashire coal field. These are disadvantages; but on the other hand, it is situated a little outside the thoroughly manufacturing area, and, therefore, commands the first offer of the services of a continually immigrating surplus agricultural population. Its markets, from the same cause, being better supplied, provisions are consequently cheaper. This is demonstrated by the prevailing practice of many farmers in the neighbourhood, who regularly transfer their produce to Blackburn, Bolton, etc., simply because, by so doing, they obtain better prices. These circumstances, added to the acknowledged fact, that Preston is a more desirable place of residence than most other neighbouring towns, will explain why the manufacturing capitalists require a somewhat lower rate of wages to compete with the general trade; and, likewise, how they continue so to rule it, notwithstanding the severe struggles consequent upon its supposed injustice.

The most important struggle between labour and capital commenced in 1853. In the earlier half of the year, the exports of the kingdom had risen to £41,866,557, against £33,549,392, showing an increase of £8,317,165. The prices of provisions were very high, and although this does not materially affect the rate of wages, it unquestionably stimulated the operatives in their demands. Strikes were pretty general throughout the country. The workmen triumphed at Stockport and other places. The flame at length spread to Preston. The operatives contended that they were entitled to 'the ten per cent. which was taken off in 1842, and also the ten per cent. taken from them in 1847-8, and if the manufacturers were men of their word they would not scruple to give it according to their promise.' Ten per cent. advance, accordingly was the war cry. This was, at first, partially conceded, but some difficulties arose as to its practical adjustment in two or three mills. An attempt was made by the operatives to assimilate the rates of remuneration in the various mills, taking the most favourable, of course, as the standard. This caused a strike in two or three establishments. The dispute eventually caused the locking up of all the mills, and a determination on the part of both employers and employed to contest the question to the uttermost. The latter were wishful to refer their differences to arbitration but the 'masters' declined all interference with their business arrangements.

Several meetings were held in the 'Orchard' during August; and by the end of the month, the hands in four or five establishments, either entirely or partially agreed to 'strike'. At the end of September, about a dozen mills were closed by the employers. This policy was soon afterwards adopted by the remainder of the establishments in Preston and the neighbourhood, with a very few exceptions. This constituted the 'lock-out'. The struggle lasted till nearly the end of May, in the following year. The commercial prosperity, which heralded the strife, had passed away, and the workmen were compelled to resume their employment on the masters' terms. The affairs of the operatives were managed by two distinct committees, one representing the spinners, and the other the power-loom weavers. The greatest distress was felt by the remainder of the hands unemployed; many of whom did not wish to suspend labour, as they were not in a position to claim relief from the funds of any union. The total number of hands thrown out of employment, has been variously estimated at from 20,000 to 26,000...

The Preston strikes have furnished valuable material for future reflection, but they have not yet evolved a practical principle, calculated to put an end to such struggles. The passage from serfdom to perfect freedom has not yet been accomplished. The victory obtained by the employers merely demonstrated that which every one previously knew, viz., the strongest party in the end would win. But this is not sufficient to set at rest the mighty question, which yearly throbs with increased vitality beneath the surging mass of mercantile contention. No one really wins in these struggles. They are essentially productive of loss to all, except in so far as they inculcate lessons of wisdom. It is, therefore, the duty and interest of all, that the differences which must occur occasionally between the buyers and sellers of labour, as well as of any other commodity, should be settled in a commercial, and not in a military spirit. (G. Hardwick, *History of the borough of Preston*, 1857.)

Carpet weaver

Bate: reduce. Temple: instrument for stretching cloth on loom. Stud: support (?). Him: the employer.

Opposite: This ballad dates from 1853, a year in which there were many strikes (including another one of carpet weavers at Kidderminster). At Preston, the weavers went on strike for an increase of 10%, which was to have restored a reduction of 10% which they had agreed to, some years earlier. The employers refused to give in, and shut down all the mills. The strike and lock-out lasted for nine months. During the dispute, Charles Dickens visited Preston and used his observations in the novel, *Hard Times* (published 1854).

Song 12   *The Coventry weaver*

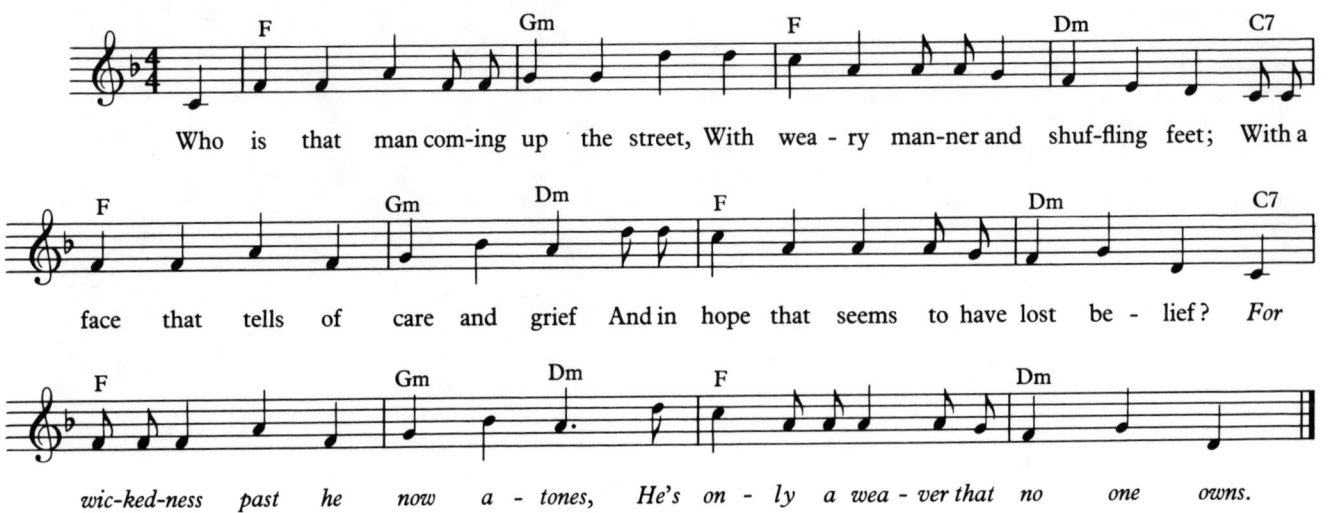

Who is that man coming up the street, With weary manner and shuffling feet; With a face that tells of care and grief And in hope that seems to have lost belief? For wickedness past he now atones, He's only a weaver that no one owns.

2 He's coming no doubt from breaking stones,
   With saddened heart and aching bones;
   But why should he grumble, he gets good pay:
   A loaf and sixpence every day.

3 He thought if he worked both night and day,
   He ought to receive equivalent pay;
   But he's just an inconsistent man,
   Who don't understand the commercial plan.

4 Political economy now must sway
   And say when a man shall work or play.
   If he's wanted his wages may be high;
   If he isn't, why then, he may starve and die.

5 If you employ him, don't mend the price –
   He's starving, you know, and has no choice –
   And give him to weave the worst of silk,
   For it's only a weaver's time you bilk.

6 Give him likewise the weighted shute –
   It's only his winding account you loot –
   And he may, perhaps, when his warps are out,
   Be minus a pound to put him about.

7 Though he use a new pattern and has to pay
   For compensator, harness and slay;
   Though he lose two weeks in anxious toil,
   And has to pay for the steam the while.

8 Though he often plays for the want of shute,
   And has plenty of knock-downs to boot;
   Though threads come down from the roll in scores,
   And a hundred other disasters more.

9 Yet take no heed of his sighs and groans,
   His careworn face, his agonised moans;
   For wickedness past he now atones,
   He's only a weaver that no one owns.

Bilk: cheat. Weighted shute: possibly, weighted shuttle, which slowed down the work, and thus reduced earnings. Compensator, harness and slay: components of the loom. Plays: stands idle. Want of shute: possibly, lack of prepared shuttles. Knock-downs: break-downs.

Distress among the Coventry ribbon weavers, 1860-1

...trade declined, and wages came down rapidly. This the weavers in a body resisted, and the struggle culminated in the terrible strike and lock-out of 1860-1. It is computed that nearly 14,000 people were at that time dependent upon the silk trade in Coventry and district, and the consequence of this dispute was that all looms, whether on hire or purchase, were called in by the manufacturers, who were in a great measure determined not to give in to the demands of their hands, but were determined to compel them to work for weekly wages on the factory system.

This strike and lock-out, combined with the cessation of the fashion of wearing ribbons, in the course of a few years reduced the number of Coventry manufacturers from eighty to less than twenty, and caused a decrease in the population of the city of over five thousand. Hundreds of looms, the first cost of which was from £40 to £100, were sold to brokers for a mere song to enable weavers to obtain the means to sustain life, and were ultimately broken up for what the wood and metal would realise. The new loom upon which I had bestowed so much trouble was called in and placed in a factory, and I was out of employment for more than a year...

During this period we subsisted upon the little capital saved during more prosperous times. Eventually, as with many others, the last penny was spent, with no prospect of obtaining another meal. At this juncture my younger brother came to inquire how we were getting on, and found my wife in tears, and myself half mad through not being able to work (owing to physical incapacity) with other distressed weavers on the common lands for sixpence and a quartern loaf per day...

Such a general state of extreme poverty was never known in Coventry before. Many weavers with large families were compelled to make raids upon the field camps of turnips and potatoes to save their children from utter starvation. The Workhouse was filled to overflowing; the rates went up enormously to supply the out-door poor with a scanty pittance; shopkeepers were on the verge of ruin, and no credit could be obtained for food; the manufacturers one after another were going into bankruptcy, and nearly eight hundred houses were soon without tenants. Hundreds of families emigrated by means of help to America and the Colonies, and at home, besides the relief works on the commons, soup kitchens were opened to appease the famished people who could not get bread. A sheet of verses was circulated through the town, composed by Thomas Rushton, a compositor on the *Coventry Herald*, a parody of Tom Hood's poem *The Pauper*. This song was sung by bodies of distressed weavers, who marched in procession through the streets, or when they proceeded to and from their work on the commons. (Joseph Gutteridge, *Lights and shadows in the life of an artisan*, 1893.)

Employment of Lancashire operatives, under the Public Works Act, at Revidge Hill, Corporation Park, Blackburn, January 1864

Song 13 *Nailers' song*

'Om-mer, 'om-mer, 'om-mer, click, clink, clink, Work all day with-out a-ny drink;
Pud-ding on a Sun-day with-out a-ny fat: Poor old nail-ers can't buy that.

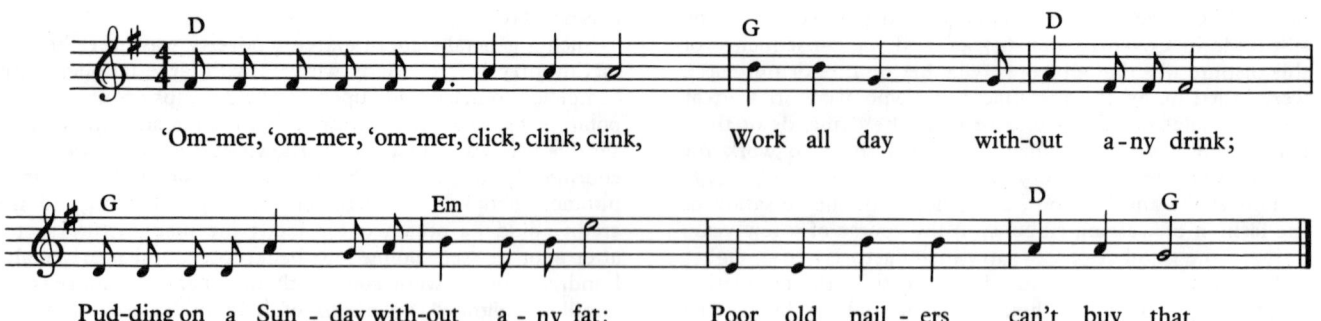

Wolverhampton, 1866

'Ommer: hammer.

The making of nails by hand was carried on in various parts of England, including the Black Country, whence this song comes. Much of the industry was carried on in back-street workshops, often in squalid conditions. After about 1830, the hand-made nail trade declined, as machine-made nails increased in number. Many nailers turned to chain-making, again in back-street workshops or small factories. This trade continued until the twentieth century. Both nails and chain were often made by women (cf. song No. 19).

Song 14 *The nailmakers' strike*

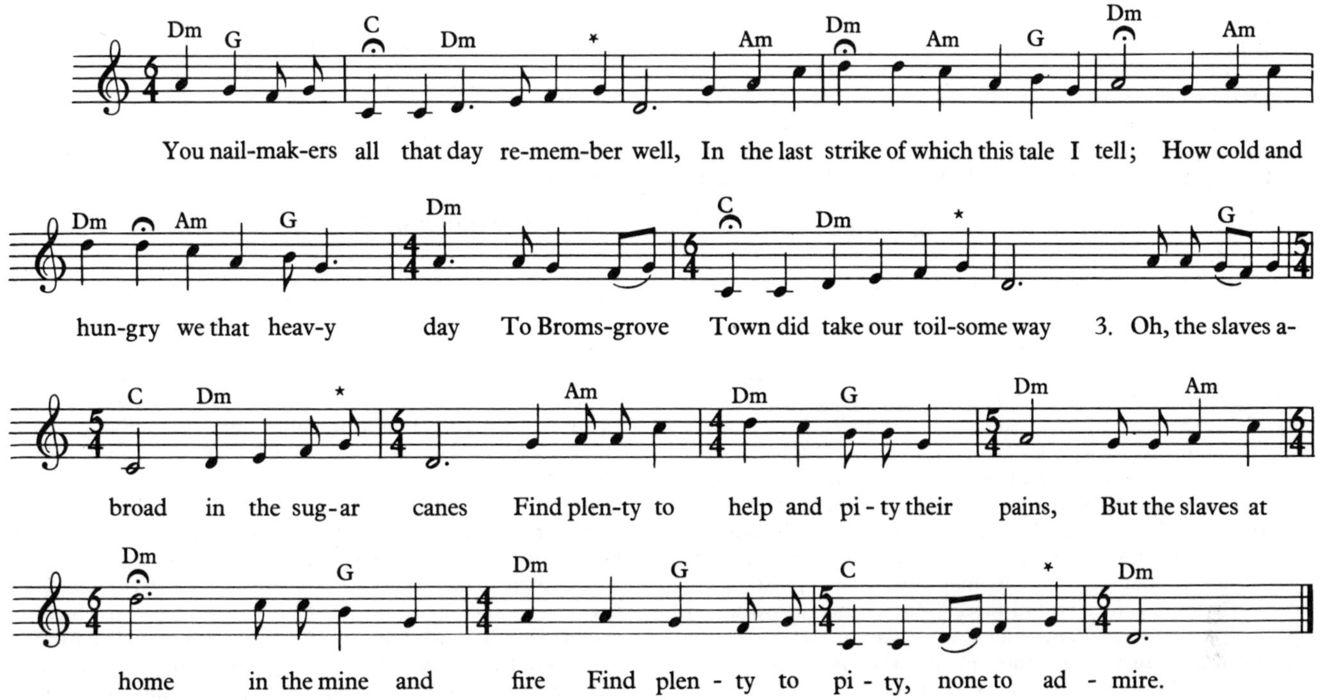

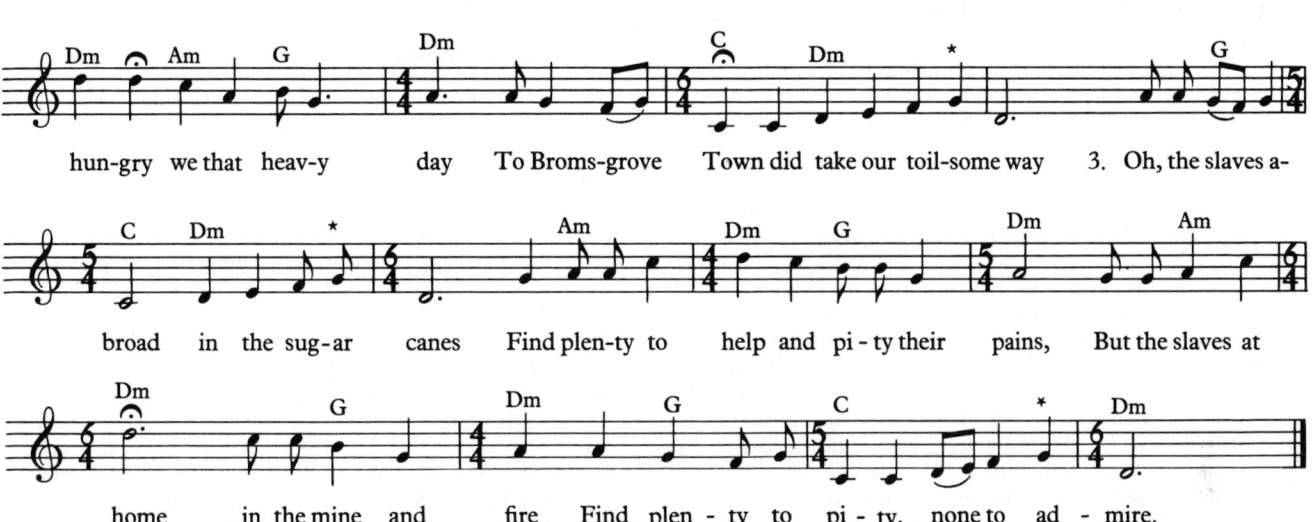

2 And those nail-forgers, miserable souls,
   Will not forget the giver of the coals.
   Nailmasters are hard-hearted files –
   The way we took was thirteen miles.

3 Oh, the slaves abroad in the sugar canes
   Find plenty to help and pity their pains,
   But the slaves at home in the mine or fire
   Find plenty to pity, none to admire.

4 Oh, I wish I could see all nail dealers
   Draw such a load as did we poor nailers,
   And to feel such punishment and such smarts,
   That it may soften their hard, stony hearts.

5 So as the nailers do suffer such smarts,
   I hope it will soften Pharoah's heart;
   Let every nailer tell to his son
   The labours that we for just rights have done.

* This note omitted in some verses.

Bromsgrove: in Worcestershire. Many of the nailmasters lived there. Thirteen miles: the distance from Halesowen to Bromsgrove, which was the route taken by the demonstration.

During a strike of nailers in 1862, partly against truck (see pp. 28 and 61), and partly against low prices, a protest march was held. Led by Sam Salt, broker, general dealer, bookseller and poet, the nailers marched from Halesowen to Bromsgrove, pulling a ton of coal which had been donated by a well-wisher. This was sold at Bromsgrove for the benefit of the strike fund. Sam Salt also published a poem of 105 verses to uphold the nailers' cause (see p. 28).

An additional difficulty for the nailers was that they often had to deal with middle men, called foggers. It is still said in the Black Country that foggers had three pairs of scales: the first, used when the iron was weighed out for the nailers, gave under the weight shown; the second, used when the nailers brought their finished nails to be weighed, weighed light; the third was accurate, and was used if inspectors of weights and measures called.

The nailers' strike 1862-3

April 5th. The Truck System: On Tuesday morning last between two and three hundred of the nailers of the town and neighbourhood assembled in the Cattle Market for the purpose of denouncing the truck system. Mr D. Banner of Catshill, having been appointed president...[said] the object of the meeting was...to protest and wage war against the truck system, which was doubly injurious to the working classes, as not only did the truck master get an undue profit upon the provisions sold by him, forcing his workmen to buy indirectly bacon from him at 10*d* per lb which could be bought equally as good at the general shops for 6*d* per lb, and other articles in the same proportion, but lowered wages; for having thus secured a large profit, he could, in the disposal of his nails, afford to sell under the regular masters.

April 12th. The Nailers' Strike: The nailers' strike appears to be more general than it has ever previously been; about 13,000 being now out. At Old Hill, Halesowen, the Lye, and Rowley, the manufacture of common nails has entirely ceased, and but little work is being done at Dudley. Large meetings of those on strike have been held during the week, especially at Old Hill, and the general determination come to is not to resume work till the old prices are given. The masters have confirmed their expressed intention of reducing the price list 10 per cent...The majority of the masters are perfectly willing to give full prices, but cannot do so under present circumstances, inasmuch as they are undersold in the market by those who get their goods at 10 per cent less. A meeting of those on strike was held on Wednesday last at the Old Hill; there were about a thousand present. A man named Priest took the chair; he said that having been among the nailmakers of the district, he was enabled to assure the meeting that the men were determined to stand firm until all the masters had agreed to pay the full price. Some workmen could only earn 10*s* or 11*s* a week, even if they worked hard, and yet they were asked to consent to a reduction on that amount of 20 per cent or more, so that 20*s* only represented 15*s* 6*d* or 16*s*. A resolution was passed by which the assembly agreed not to return to work until the full price was paid.

August 1st 1863. Nailmasters' Meeting: At a meeting of the nailmasters, held yesterday (Friday) evening...it was unanimously resolved: 'That in order to put a stop to the distress that exists, the men be offered the opportunity of returning to their work at the 20*s* rate for a period of two months; with the understanding that in the meantime they endeavour to induce the masters in the up-districts to pay the same. Should the up-district masters decline to do so, the Bromsgrove masters will then reduce to what they are paying.'

August 8th. Termination of the Nailers' Strike: The resolution passed by the nailmasters on Friday last...has led to the termination of the strike.

[Extracts from the *Bromsgrove and Droitwich Weekly Messenger*.]

Halesowen nailers, 1869

The sun was fast declining in the west, so there was less time than I could have wished for visiting these little domestic workshops. We called in at one, however, and had a long talk with the woman at her anvil. Her husband was a collier, and she alone carried on the nail-making in the little shop, which is an apartment or addendum to every nailer's house as much as his kitchen. She could only be four days of the week at the forge, because, as she said, she had to 'fettle' about the house, washing and mending for the family and doing other wife's work. She could only earn between three and four shillings a week at the anvil; but that was a great help to them, and helped out her husband's wages.

The nail-maker pays on an average 2*s* 6*d* a week for his cottage and shop. He must find his own tools, which are rather simple and few in number...The nail-master or merchant furnishes the iron in bundles to the nail-maker, weighing sixty pounds each, and allows him from six to twenty-eight pounds for waste per bundle, according to the size of the nails; the largest size, or course, wasting less iron per pound produced...

The hand-made nail trade has been sadly depressed for nearly half a century and from various causes. First, the competition with machinery has greatly diminished the production of the hammer, as well as depressed its price. In 1830 it was estimated that about 50,000 persons were employed in the manufacture; whereas, the present number thus employed is put at 20,000. The earnings of a family of man, wife, son or daughter will possibly average about twenty shillings per week, out of which they must pay for their coal, and the extra rent charged for their shop...The nailers have 'struck' for higher wages frequently, and endeavoured to win them by virtue of self-imposed suffering; but apparently in this age of machinery and cheaper foreign labour, there is but little improvement possible. (Elihu Burritt, *Walks in the Black Country*, 1869.)

Some verses from Sam Salt's poem.

The nailers are now again on the strike,
Through being served with such tricks they don't like.
Nailers have been on strike for many weeks:
This is caused through the masters' shameful tricks.

But if the strike lasts long I do dread
Many poor children will cry out for bread.

Oh how hard when children are took to bed
For them to say, 'Oh, mother, we want bread'.

I tell you again, keep stout then, I say,
The masters must the twenty shillings pay.
For the nails they cannot be done without,
Neither hob nails nor clinkers, nor fine clout.

Song 15 *The poor nailmaker*

From morn till night, from early light, we toil for little pay. God help the poor of Rowley throughout each weary day. There is a house in Old Hill town, a garden by its door, Where the keeper keeps you breaking stones for ever, ever more.

Rowley Regis, Old Hill: Black Country townships. A house: the workhouse.

Nailers' living conditions became a by-word for squalor. As late as 1889 a Select Committee of the House of Commons enquired into the trade. One of its witnesses was Henry Parker of Sedgley, who had been a nailer for 50 years. At one time he had earned 2*s* for a bundle of spikes. 'In 1888 he received 8*d* and his total weekly earning was 9*s*. Out of this money he had to purchase three bags of breeze [refuse from puddling furnace] at 6*d* a bag. To make some extra money he let part of his workshop to two young women of 18 and 24 years. They paid him 6*d* a week rent, and by working from 6 a.m. to 8 p.m. for five days a week were able to earn 4*s* 9*d* for working up two bundles of staples each. Another entry in the report recounts how Joseph Wilkes of Sedgley managed to keep his family of seven. He claimed that they lived mostly on tea, bread, bacon and margarine – his grocery bill for a week was 2 quarters of tea 1*s*, 4 lb of sugar 8*d*, bread 3*s*, coal 1*s* 10*d*, meat 2*s*, bacon 1*s* 6*d*.

    The necessity of working long hours for so little resulted in the nail-maker becoming socially and morally debased. The 1889 report claims 'a tidy home is exceptional' and 'immorality is caused by women working in a state of semi-dress'. It was also stated that young men chose a wife not by her looks but on her ability as a nail-maker'. (V. L. Davies and H. Hyde, *Dudley and the Black Country, 1760-1860*, 1970.)

Song 16 *Tally i o, the grinder!*

2 He shortens his life and he hastens his death,
   Will drink steel dust in every breath;
   Won't use a fan as he turns his wheel,
   Won't wash his hands ere he eats his meal,
   But dies as he lives, as hard as steel.

3 These Sheffield grinders of whom we speak
   Are men who earn a pound a week;
   But of Sheffield grinders another sort
   Methinks ought to be called in court,
   And that is the grinding Government Board.

4 At whose door lies the blacker blame?
   Where rests the heavier weight of shame?
   On the famine-price contractor's head,
   Or the workman's, under-taught and fed,
   Who grinds his own bones and his child's, for bread?

Hull: 'In a hull there may be several grinding-troughs; at each there works one grinder; he sits astride a wooden seat called a horsing, and leans forward over the grinding stone, which revolves away from him and which is kept wet by passing through water contained in a wooden trough at each revolution. The grinding hull is usually a lofty, airy place, the windows being open, and not having glass in them'. (J. Wright, *English Dialect Dictionary*.)

The Sheffield outrages

Sheffield has grown steadily in prosperity and importance in spite of the fact that times always seemed to be bad. Perhaps that is why her one period of almost uninterrupted well-being – from 1850 to 1873 – coincided with an outbreak of serious industrial troubles. The lower-paid workers naturally wanted their share of the fruits of the boom.

The root of these troubles was the question of wages – or rather, since they arose mainly in the cutlery trades, of payment; for in these trades there were large numbers of very small firms and of independent outworkers and others who hired places in a larger manufacturer's shop and sold him the goods they made. A question of not much less importance was that of the number of workers admitted to the trades, for in the cutlery business there always tended to be a surplus of labour, and it was difficult for men to negotiate for better rates of payment when labour was plentiful. In both these matters the 'little mesters' had done better under the control of the Cutlers' Company; and very soon after they had thrown off that control they began to seek the protection of trade unions, whose basic principles were not dissimilar, but whose power of protection was at that time much inferior.

Although a very grudging Act in 1825 had made it legal for workmen to meet in council to discuss wages and the conditions under which they were prepared to work, the matters they were not allowed to discuss as a body were so numerous and important that trade unions were still virtually illegal. Nevertheless, they existed, and in some places, of which Sheffield was an outstanding example, they had some strength. It must be borne in mind that in a community in which the 'little mester' was still more common than the large-scale manufacturer, the employers with whom the men had to deal were often hardly better off than themselves, and the employees were correspondingly stronger. But much of their strength was less real than apparent, mainly because there was a union for practically every process in every trade, and though there might be a high total of men in unions, there were never a great many in any single union.

Since the unions had no legal rights, and their poor position in law made it necessary for much of their business to be transacted in secret, if any of the officials were tempted to wrong-doing it was fatally easy for them to avoid detection even by their associates. These officials had no legal power to make their members pay subscriptions regularly, and in order to keep up the funds they were plainly exposed to the temptation to blackmail.

Simple blackmail – for that is what 'rattening' really was – had been practised to a certain extent in many places for a long time – indeed, it was common in the old guilds. But in Sheffield it began to assume really serious proportions as early as 1816, and by 1860 had grown to such an extent that it caused a scandal of national concern.

Rattening was easy in Sheffield, for so simple an act as removing a grinder's wheelbands brought to a standstill not merely his own work but that of the men carrying out the other processes. At first this was the only form of blackmail resorted to, and it was mild enough. Wheelbands were stolen secretly, and the offending workman informed that he must pay his arrears, or rejoin the union, or otherwise mend his ways, before they were returned. Almost invariably the bands were restored, with secrecy equal to that with which they had been taken, when the demand was met. However much the individual might object, he had no redress, for nobody 'sneaked' though everybody knew about it. The conspiracy of silence continued, even when these coercive measures took a more sinister form.

Sheffield cutler

Charges of gunpowder were put in chimney stacks and in grinding troughs; men were shot at, and their farm animals killed or wounded. Masters who employed non-union men – even specialists whose work the ordinary labourer could not do – received the same sort of unpleasant attentions, and the same threatening letters signed by 'Mary Ann'. A hidden terror began to haunt all but the most conventional and docile union members. The police hardly ever managed to convict anybody. Yet the whole body of Sheffield workmen remained silent. Many of the union officials disapproved, many men sincerely attached to the trade union movement were made uneasy by it; but they said nothing.

The writers of the letters had a pretty turn for 'black hand' composition. This was received by the directors of Firth's: 'Gentlemen: The game works merrily and we brush away all obstacles before us. If we appear to be rather long about it you see we are none the less sure. It is your turn next, and the man who pays back would be the first to get it. If I but move my finger you are sent to eternity as sure as fate. Be advised and take the hint in time.'

Under this cloak of secrecy and immunity some of the wrongdoers finally went too far. Similar happenings in Manchester brought the two towns into the limelight in a most unfortunate fashion. The whole trade union movement was being brought into disrepute, and the honourable leaders of

Cutlery – exterior view of the Castle Grinding Mill at Sheffield

the movement, no less than men of standing who had no connection with industry, were seriously disturbed.

Two very bad cases brought matters to a head. In 1859 James Linley was killed by a shot from an air gun. In 1861, gunpowder was lighted in the house of George Wastnidge; a woman lodger was burnt so badly that she died, and Wastnidge's wife, who tried to help her, was ill for a long time as a result of her own burns. Men of influence began to bestir themselves.

In 1864 William Christopher Leng came to Sheffield to take over part proprietorship of the *Sheffield Telegraph*. For some reason (perhaps because he came fresh to the problem) he was the only one to suspect the man who was afterwards unmasked as the worst of the leading spirits. He could only hint, for he had no evidence. He threw himself into agitation with his characteristic fighting spirit, critical faculty, and disregard of consequences, and he was largely instrumental in getting a Royal Commission appointed 'to enquire into the organization and rules of trade unions, with power to investigate any recent acts of intimidation, outrage or wrong alleged to have been promoted, encouraged, or connived at by such trade unions.'

The Royal Commission, unable to do anything in London about the position in Sheffield, appointed William Overend, Q.C., Thomas Irwin Barstow and George Chance to be local examiners. They began their investigations on June 3rd, 1867.

The conspiracy of silence continued. The examiners soon found that nobody would speak unless complete immunity was promised. This highly injudicial, but in the circumstances, prudent, course was adopted.

The enquiry began quietly; but as day after day the evidence mounted, as witnesses with immunity certificates spoke more freely and their statements began to border on the sensational, excitement and tension grew. At length, the evidence began to point towards one who had sat in smug security, looking like a shocked spectator anxious to see justice done. Leng, who alone had suspected him, was guarded night and day by three constables.

John Jackson, Sheffield's most famous Chief Constable, was ultimately responsible for the unmasking. He concentrated on a wretched little man called Hallam, whom he in turn persuaded by kindness, comforted by tact, and intimidated by spells of solitary confinement. Which of these methods was really responsible for Hallam's breakdown is in question, but, whether it was in fear of, or liking for, the man who stood by him through his ordeal in the dock, Hallam did break down completely. He fainted more than once; but his confession unmasked as the principal wrongdoer one William Broadhead, saw grinder, landlord of the Royal George Inn, Carver Street, and Treasurer of the Associated Trades of Sheffield.

When the scoundrel Broadhead (for there is no doubt he deserved no better epithet) was called to give evidence he had the saving grace not to implicate the innocent. He stated that his colleagues on the Saw Grinders' Union Committee knew nothing about it, and that he had falsified the books so that he could pay in secret the men who worked for him, one of whom he had sent to the United States. (One of the factors in emigration at this period is amply illustrated by the remark of a former Sheffield man who met a steel magnate coming off the ship at New York, 'Why, Tom, what hast *tha* done amiss?')

Never was patient and successful enquiry into crime so curiously ended. The immunity certificates were honoured; the examiners quietly withdrew, and issued a report so plain, and so unbiassed, that in reading it one has to make an effort to realise the nagging anxieties, the conflict of wills, the real loss and suffering which had been caused by men like Broadhead.

After recording the facts of the proved cases, they reported that of the sixty trade unions in Sheffield, twelve only had resorted to outrage; that in these unions the majority of members had been quite unaware of the guilt of their officials; that in the period under review, no employers' associations had been guilty of such crimes. Although some of the outrages had been the work of the fender-grinders, the pen and pocket blade grinders, the scissor forgers, the scissor grinders, the edge tool grinders and the scythe grinders, the longest list of crimes was brought home to the saw grinders at the instigation of Broadhead.

Broadhead went to the United States (he returned later in life). Samuel Crookes, who had been responsible under his direction for blowing up Wheatman and Smith's saw factory, and who had been jointly responsible with Hallam for the death of James Linley, remained at home, and the Rev. Robert Stainton, a Congregational minister who incurred unpopularity by his championship of the man, secured from his former employers a promise to take him back. Crookes justified his sincerely Christian impulse, and the trust of his employers, and sinned no more.

The Commissioners in London presented a report, and a minority report was added by Thomas Hughes* and Frederic Harrison. It was the minority report which had most effect upon the Trade Union Act of 1871 which legalised the Unions. The abandonment of secrecy had a very healthy effect, and serious outrages no longer brought the name of Sheffield into disrepute.

Rattening did not, however, altogether cease, and though violence was over, unrest remained. This is not the place to attempt any survey of the trade union movement in general but it is well known how the struggle for better wages and shorter hours continued in all trades, and how the scales tilted this way and that as new troubles arose in the commercial world. (M. Walton, *Sheffield, its story and its achievements*, 1968.)

*Author of *Tom Brown's Schooldays*.

Sheffield scythe tilters

Song 17 *Joe, the factory lad*

2 Now I was born in Manchester, in Ancoats Lane was reared,
   And brought up as a factory lad, I was, upon my word;
   I never fret for what I can't get, you'll never find me sad,
   I know there's many worse off than me, the honest factory lad.

3   We factory lads have been on strike to get nine hours a day;
    Not only that, but we require a little extra pay.
    And then to work we'll proudly go – each one will feel so glad –
    I'm sure there's none can feel more so than Joe, the factory lad.

4   Although I lead a jolly life, I always like to see
    My friends around, good-tempered like, and just the same as me;
    Then merrily we'll jog along without a care, I know:
    No one could lead a happier life than little factory Joe.

In 1850 the hours of work in textile mills were limited by law to ten per day. This provision was extended to other industries in 1875. The Factory Act of 1878 reduced hours of work further, to nine. The eight-hour day and the five-day week were not, of course, achieved in Britain until after the second world war.

Song 18 *The matchgirls' song*

Members of the Matchmakers Union, 1888

When they went on strike they walked through Bow, all the way up Mile End Road, Whitechapel Road and Leadenhall Street, and straight through to Trafalgar Square. And on the way through Leadenhall Street particularly they used to sing [to the tune of *John Brown's Body*]:

We'll hang old Bryant on a sour apple tree,
We'll hang old Bryant on a sour apple tree,
We'll hang old Bryant on a sour apple tree,
As we go marchin' in.
Glory, glory, hallelujah, glory, glory, hallelujah,
Glory, glory, hallelujah,
As we go marchin' in.

And while they were walking along, the people in the offices overhead would throw some coppers [coins] down; and then there'd be a scramble among the girls to get these coppers up. That caused a bit of an interlude from the singing; and when they'd picked up all the coppers, on they'd go again, singing and marching. (Recollections of Mr Samuel Webber, in an interview with Roy Palmer, 1971. Mr Webber was born in 1874.)

In 1888 the match girls from Bryant and May's factory in the East End of London organised a successful strike for the right to organise themselves into a union. In the following year, there was a strike, by the dockers, for a minimum wage of sixpence an hour: the docker's tanner, as it was called. This was also largely successful.

Song 19 *Holly ho*

I'll sing you a song, a pe-cu-li-ar song, And if you will lis-ten it won't take me long. The

rhyme's ve-ry pret-ty, I'm sure you'll a-gree, And no doubt you'll all sing this chor-us with me. Hol-ly

ho, ———— hol-ly ho, ———— Fol the whack dol the doo-dle da day. ————

2 I said to my sweetheart the other day,
   'What do you want for your birthday?'
   She answered, 'Diamonds', and straight there and then,
   I gave her the Ace, the King, Queen, Jack and ten.

3 The lady chainmakers have all gone on strike;
   The gaffers they think they can pay what they like;
   They work 'em so hard both by night and by day,
   And for it they all get such terrible pay.

4 I dreamt that I died and to heaven did go;
   'Where do you come from?', they wanted to know.
   When I said, 'From Cradley', well, how they did stare;
   They said, 'Come right in, lad, you're the first chap from there'.

5 My brother bought a cow, but then poorly it fell,
   So we fed it on rum, just to make it get well;
   And just like the silk-worm that gives us the silk,
   That cow gives my brother hot rum and milk.

6 Now me and — — —*, we're all right, you see,
   And when we go out, we go out on the spree;
   And whether we win or whether we lose,
   We're always ready for a drop of good booze.

7 I brought me a chicken from town yesterday,
   I thought that for me a nice egg it would lay.
   Well, early this morning I had a great shock,
   The fowl says, 'I can't lay an egg, I'm a cock'.

* Insert appropriate name

This song was sung within living memory in Black Country chain-making shops. On pay-day, some one would start off with 'his' verse, and others would contribute their own favourite verses, with everyone joining in the chorus.

   The strike of lady chainmakers mentioned in verse 3 took place in 1910 at Cradley Heath, formerly in Staffordshire.

The striking lady chainmakers after a distribution of bread at Cradley, in 1910

A lady chainmaker, 1970

Mrs Lucy Woodall, of Old Hill, Warley, Worcestershire, was still working as a chainmaker in 1970, at the age of 71, having started 58 years earlier. She remembered the practical jokes played on her at the time: 'They'd say: "Goo and fetch that left-'anded spanner". Alternatively, they would hide the tools or 'heat the tongs at the wrong end to make you jump'. She continued:

Them days were happier – tougher, but far happier. They'd all mix up together, where they wouldn't today. No happiness today – well, not in factories. They seem to be nasty and jealous o' one another.

When I started first in 1912 I was only 13. I left school on the Friday and I started on the Monday. Four shillin' a week. Seven o'clock till seven o'clock. Two o'clock on a Saturday. Well, when you start first they get you doin' a bit o' blowin' for one of the others to kind o' break yer in a bit. And then after that you start tryin' to turn a link and then you go on to shuttin' a link.

You was glad to do it. There was no work really in them days. I had to do six month, you know, at that four shillin'. And then the next six month I 'ad a rise – five and six. 'Course, I had to do two years as apprentice. Then the next twelve months I 'ad nine shillin', but they gave yer a stint work for that nine shillin'. Well, when you'd done that stint, if you did any extra that was put on one side every day and you was paid piece work on that little bit. Well, sometimes I should have two shillin' or half a crown and I should be in 'eaven. And then after you'd done your apprenticeship you 'ad piece work – different sorts. Different sizes.

There was one or two started, like, as the same time as me. And one of 'em, I remember 'er. The boss'd 'ad an order come in for No.6 – and that was about eight link to the foot, I think. 'Er says, 'A bay [I'm not] a-bloody-mekin' that', 'er says. 'A s'll 'a' [I shall have] to mek a bloody ton to weigh 'undredweight.' I remember that. (Mrs Lucy Woodall, in an interview with Roy Palmer, 1970.)

2
Pit life: down among the coal

Pit, 1870

Here's just a swatch of pitmen's life,
Frae bein' breek'd till fit te marry:
A scene o' senseless pain and strife,
Hatch'd by wor deedly foe, AWD HARRY:

For there's ne imp iv a' his hell
That could sic tortur hev invented:
It mun ha'e been AWD NICKY's sel –
He likes te see us se tormented.

Then ye that sleep on beds o' doon,
An' niver JACK THE CALLER dreedin' –
Gan finely clad the hyell year roun',
And a'ways upon dainties feedin' –

Think on us, hinnies, if ye please,
An it were but te show yor pity;
For a' the toils and tears it gi'es,
Te warm the shins o' Lunnun city.

The fiery 'blast' cuts short wor lives,
And steeps wor hyems in deep distress,
Myeks widows o' wor canny wives,
And a' wor bairns leaves faitherless.

The wait'ry 'wyest', mair dreedful still,
Alive oft barries huz belaw:
O dear! it myeks yen's blood run chill!
May we sic mis'ry niver knaw!

(*The pitman's pay*, 1828).
A swatch is a sample. Wyest is waste.

Song 20 *Down the pit we want to go*

Down the pit we want to go, A-way from school with all its woe; Work-ing hard as col-lier's but-ty* Make us all so ve-ry hap-py! Did you ev-er see, did you ev-er see, Did you ev-er see such a fun-ny thing be-fore?

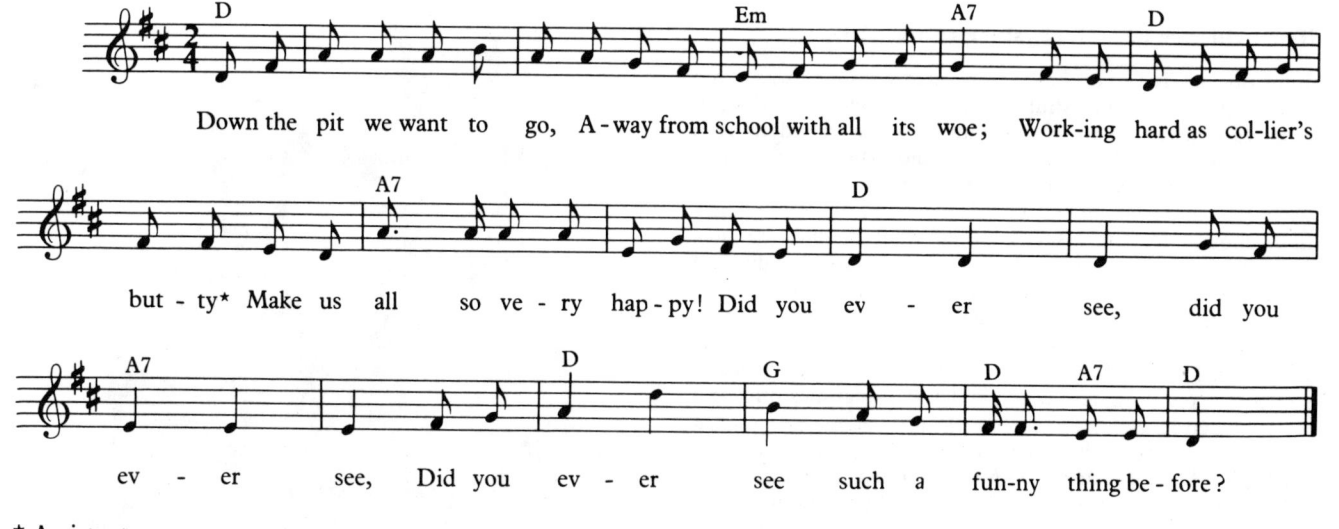

* Assistant

Song 21 *Working today*

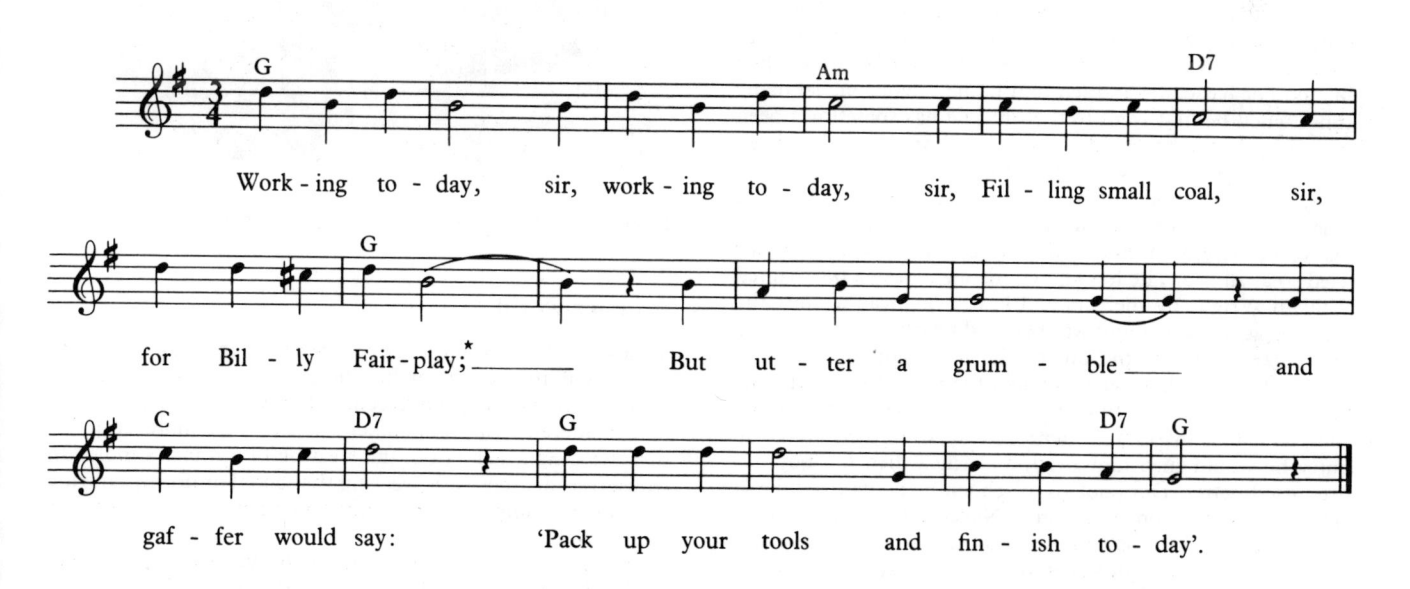

Work-ing to-day, sir, work-ing to-day, sir, Fil-ling small coal, sir, for Bil-ly Fair-play;* But ut-ter a grum-ble and gaf-fer would say: 'Pack up your tools and fin-ish to-day'.

This was sung by South Wales miners, but some very similar words were sung in Yorkshire, as part of *The pony driver* (Song no. 22):
Workin' all day, lad, for five bob a day,
Little snap time, lad, and little pay;
And if tha grumbles deputy'll say:
'Put on thi coit, lad, tha's finished the day'.

Snap: food. Coit: coat.

*Billy Fairplay was Sir William T. Lewis, the first Lord Merthyr, said to have been called by Sidney and Beatrice Webb 'the best hated man in the Principality'. As chairman of the Colliery Owners' Association of South Wales and Monmouthshire, he was almost inevitably unpopular with the miners. 'Billy Fairplay' was in itself sarcastic, but many miners preferred to substitute 'Billy Foulplay' when singing. (Information supplied by Mr Walter Haydn Davies.)

The evidence of a Derbyshire miner, 1842

John Bostock is 17 years old; he worked before he was seven years old; opened and shut the door, and had 6d a-day; in two years he began to waggon, he then was raised to 10d; when he was 11 he had 1s; at Sunderland, where he remained five years, it was not near so hard work as at Babbington; when he came back he had 1s 6d a-day, and made the banks high enough for the asses; he then went behind; he now waggons and has 2s per day; he goes down at six to eight, and sometimes the butties make them work until nine. Has to walk two miles to his work; has never more than half an hour, but seldom so much allowed for dinner, what he gets besides he is forced to snatch as he can; he has meat and potatoes and sometimes pudding, and water to drink, sometimes milk and water; when he gets home he has meat or bacon. Never work over-hours or by-night; some lads do to assist in cleaning the banks. The pit is dry both over and under; it is always hot enough to make them sweat. When they get their dinner it is very cold, 'but they soon sweaten again'; never work on Sundays; they often get their ears pulled by the corporals, and sometimes they mark their backs; they used, when his father was not with him, to take the burning candlewicks, after the tallow was off, to grease the wheels, light them and burn his arms, and has often been made to work until he was so tired as to lay down on his road home until 12 o'clock, when his mother has come and led him home – has done so many times when he first went to the pits; he has sometimes been so fatigued that he could not eat his dinner, but has been beaten and made to work until night; he never thought of play, was always too anxious to get to bed; is sure this is all true. His father works in the same pit and he is now able to do his work, therefore is not so ill used; he has known other lads used so at Ilkiston; he has known his uncle take a boy named William Wright by the ears and knock his head against the wall, because his eyesight was bad and he could not see to do his work so well as the others; he has complained to the butties, but they have always taken the part of the corporal; he has known one boy beaten until he was black and blue; he complained to Messrs Potter's agent, who then told the butty he would turn him away, and since then the boy has been used better. Does not go to school, he is too tired, he is always glad 'to stop a whoam'. Never goes to church or chapel, neither does his father or mother; he has two brothers work in the pit. His brothers go to a Sunday-school at the Ranters. Thinks a pit-boy has very hard work, and had rather work above ground, for he is sure no master dare make them work so hard where they could be seen; he is sure no boy ought to work in a pit before he is 13 years old; when he was under he has hardly known how to lie on his bed; he was tired all over, and when he has sat down he hardly knew how to get up; the belt has often made his hips quite raw. (First report of the commission on the employment of children, 1842.)

Woman and young miner of Pontypool, about 1868

A man's world

To a schoolboy there was a prestige about entering this man's world. Off to the pit on his 'first morning' he felt just as elated as the new pupil proceeding to the grammar school, for he considered wearing a collier's red muffler more desirable than wearing a school tie, the wearing of a miner's moleskin trousers as distinctive as wearing the school uniform, carrying the miner's lamp as more significant than that of carrying a school satchel.

During his last few months at school the boy's mind would be dominated by thoughts of life in the mine. He would see those of his friends who had left school swagger forth in the evenings sporting their shining silver pieces. He listened to their big talk of the events of the day, their association with men and boys at the mine, the nature of their work, the fun they had during their lunch breaks repeating the jokes and yarns they had heard and altogether extolling the spirit of camaraderie that there prevailed. (Walter Haydn Davies, *The right place, the right time*, 1972.)

Song 22 *The pony driver*

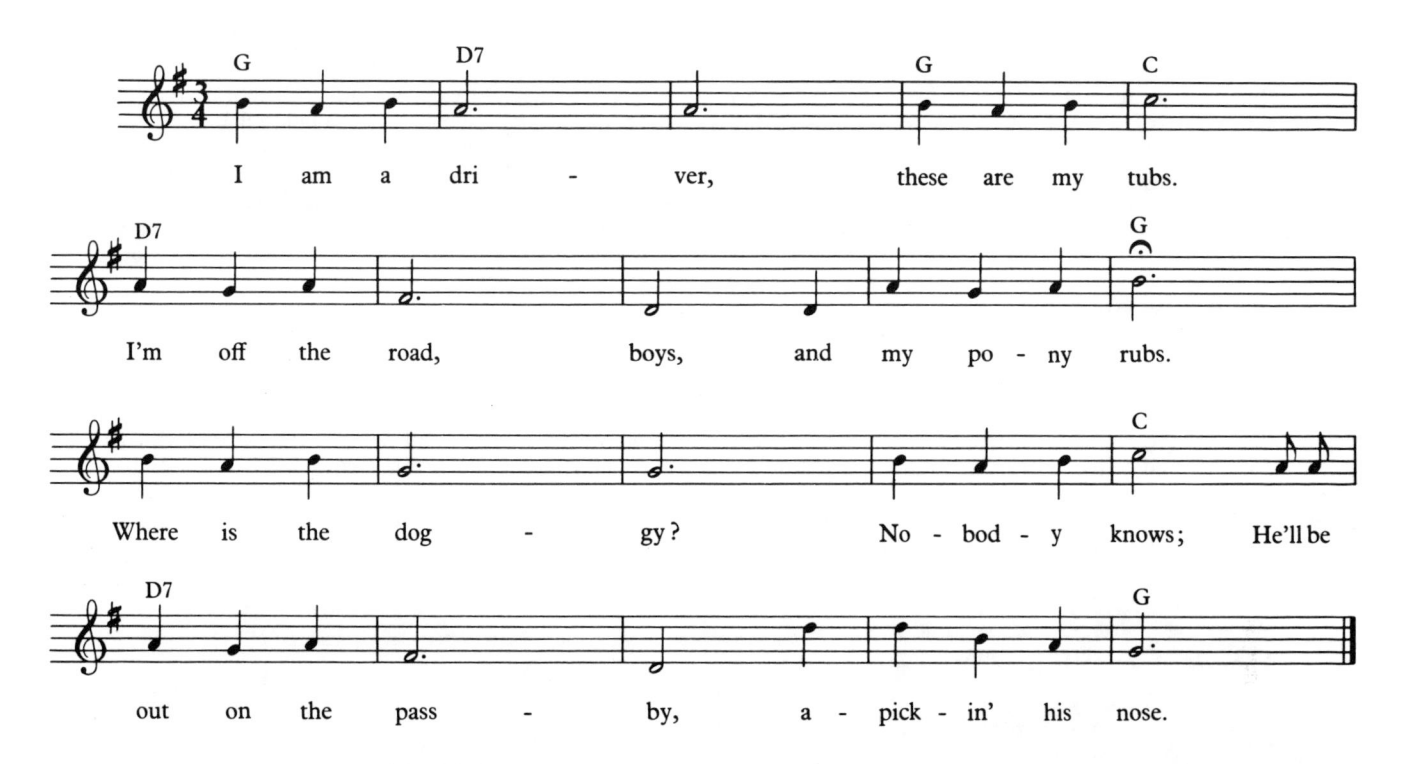

I am a driver, these are my tubs.
I'm off the road, boys, and my pony rubs.
Where is the doggy? Nobody knows;
He'll be out on the pass-by, a-pickin' his nose.

2 I shall be glad when this shift is done,
Then I'll be up there, out in the sun.
Tha'll be dahn 'ere, boy, in this dark 'oil,
Still gruntin' and groanin', pullin' this coil.

3 Corn's in the manger, water's in t'trough;
Tha'll shove thi nose out when tha's 'ad enough.
I'll tek thee in t'standin' and drop off thi gear;
When I come back, lad, I know tha'll be 'ere.

This song was collected in 1966 by A. E. Green from a Castleford miner, William Hill. Mr Hill started work in the Yorkshire pits as a pony driver at the age of fifteen. 'It was then', says Mr Green, 'that he learned this song, which the drivers would sing to their ponies, sitting on the five- and seven-hundredweight coal-tubs with their feet on the swingletrees. A 'doggy' was an overman who was responsible for maintaining the rails on which the tubs ran; it was not unusual for tubs to go off the 'road', and it was then that the doggy's job was to get them back on – if he was to be found. The 'pass-by' was a section of double track where tubs could pass, most of the road being single track. The 'standing' in verse 3 is a pony-stall. Mr Hill says that in every pit he ever worked, the stalls were marked with the pony's names, and the first five were invariably as follows: TOM/KING/SHOT/DICK/TURPIN. The business of going off the road (especially if, as here, the pony was 'rubbing', i.e. catching its back on the roof, causing an unpleasant sore), was clearly very trying to a young lad on his first job.'

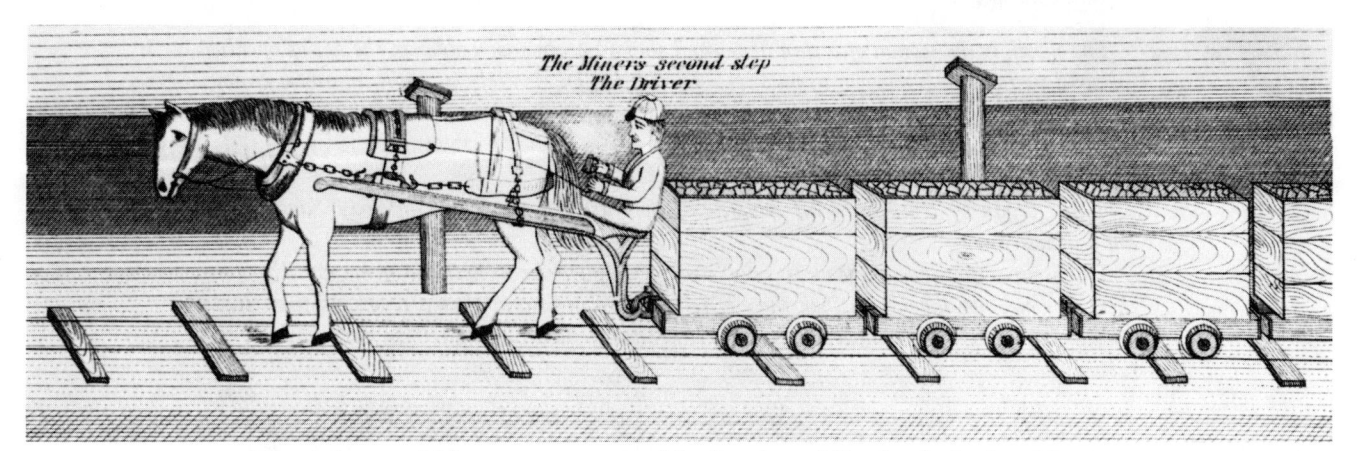

The pit horse and his gears, as was usual in the mines of Northumberland and Durham

A Durham pit boy, 1847

I commenced my underground life in Haswell Pit [Co. Durham] on November 13, 1847, the day after the completion of my tenth year...Once before I had been on a short underground visit to the pit, under the care and supervision of my father. But now, a shy, sensitive boy, I was thrown – or, rather, had voluntarily rushed – into fortune's way to take my part, as best I could, in the rough conflicts of daily pit life. The clatter, the bustle and confusion, the darkness, relieved only by the glimmering, flickering lamps, the men and boys flitting hither and thither, resembling grim shadows rather than human figures – all this seemed a fantastic dream, novel and bewildering.

To direct the air-currents of the mine, doors were placed at certain points, and it was my business to tend one of these, to open and shut it when the putters passed through on their way to the workings and on their return journey to the flat, or station. The trapper's hours...were nominally twelve, really about thirteen a day; his pay was tenpence a day, and he was expected to remain at his post the whole time in total darkness...

After working a few weeks as a trapper, I was transferred to donkey-driving. This, surely, was swift and real promotion. My pay rose at a bound from tenpence to the full round sum of a shilling a day...'Spanker' – 'Old Spanker', as he was always called – was the name of the marvellous animal committed to my charge...Spanker had all the virtues of his race – meekness, patience, forbearance...Yet I had my difficulties. Spanker would not go unless he liked – and he seldom liked. Hard work was his aversion, and yet that was precisely what he and I were appointed to do. The place where we had to 'help-up' was very steep. Its heaviest part extended only some twenty or thirty paces; but there the combined strength of the putter, pushing the tub, and Spanker pulling in front, was needed. The roadway was not only steep; it was very low and narrow...When the putter brought his full tub to the bottom of the bank, called in pit jargon the 'hitch', it was my business to attach the donkey's traces to the tub, and it was Spanker's business to pull with all his might. There was no place for me to ride, nor was there room between the tub and the donkey for me to walk, without danger. I was compelled, therefore, to go in front and lead him. My first day I shall never forget. For a while, in the early morning, Spanker buckled to with a will and did his work fairly well; but the monotony of the heavy pulling seemed to pall upon him. At length he struck work, and was immovable. (Thomas Burt [1837-1922], *Autobiography*.)

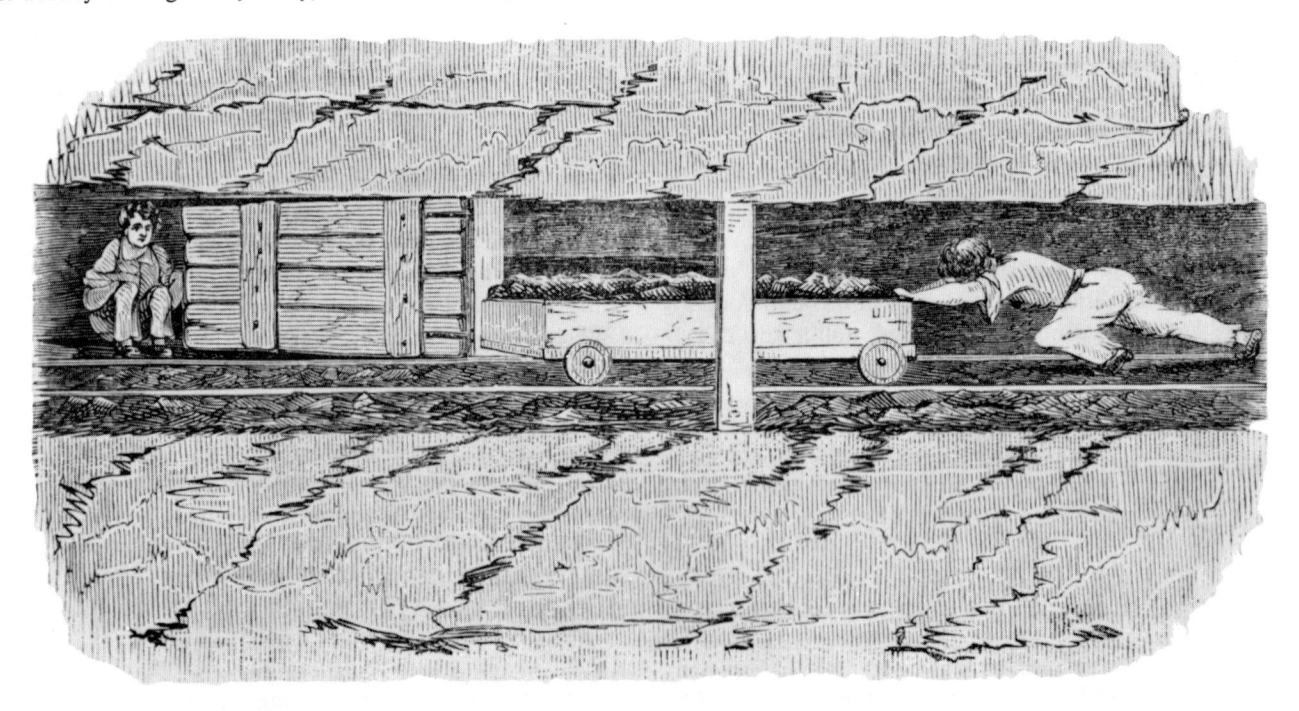

A trapper boy

The sketch is the section of a thin mine, and shows an air-door tender in the act of opening an air-door to allow a waggon to pass through. Sitting on his heels, as is the universal custom of all colliers, young and old, in this district [Lancashire]. This employment is the one to which children are generally put on first entering the mines.

A. B., at Mr. Roscoe's near Rochdale, states,

'I first began by tenting the air-doors, and then driving the Gal [Galloway], and now I am a drawer.'

This occupation is one of the most pitiable in a coal-pit, from its extreme monotony. Exertion there is none, nor labour, further than is requisite to open and shut a door. As these little fellows are always the youngest in the pits, I have generally found them very shy. (First report.)

Mining in Yorkshire and Lancashire

Mr Henry Garforth, aged 37, late book-keeper and cashier for Messrs Lees and Jones, and previously dialling (surveying) mines – Oct. 28, 1841:

Has been acquainted with the working of coals from his infancy, having commenced working at nine years of age in the neighbourhood of Wakefield, in Yorkshire. His father was manager of a colliery near Keighley, under Mr Dawson; poor and illiterate until he put himself for three years to a night-school, and by learning there to read, write, and plan, he qualified himself to be an underlooker, and take the management of a mine: this was when the witness was about five years of age. Between eight and nine years of age witness commenced to work as a trapper, being perhaps the youngest in the pit at that time. Was quite proud to begin trapping, preferring it to play; but soon got tired. Use is second nature; and for a year and a half he was a trap-door tenter without ever feeling any alarm, except when he had to go past the place where 'Old Johnson' was killed, when the mere dirt behind his feet would make him occasionally feel timid. Had the door nearest to the shaft, and was always enjoined by his father to caution; was at it 10 or 11 hours a-day. After he had done trapping, with which it was usual for the children to begin, he proceeded to the hurrying, which he looked upon as a promotion, and was proud of...

It was a five-foot seam in which he was working as a hurrier, and there was good room in the ways, in which black-damp, towards the face of the works, was sometimes very troublesome, but not the fire-damp. This hurrying was all by thrusting, and the coal lay level; but the hurrying in this country, called 'waggoning', is different, and not to be liked as he liked that. At 13 years of age he left the hurrying in Yorkshire, and came to 'waggoning' (which is the operation analogous to that of 'hurrying') at Messrs Lees, Jones, and Company's works in the neighbourhood of Oldham, in whose service he has been ever since, until two months ago – a period of nearly 25 years.

Almost the sole employment of children is as 'waggoners', 'drawers', and 'thrutchers'. The name of 'waggoners', so far from meaning that they are driving horses, describes in this locality merely what in Yorkshire is called hurrying, i.e. the loading and pushing of low waggons from the place of getting to the pit bottom. 'Drawing' consists in loading an oblong tub, measuring 27 inches long by 24 wide, and 9 high, and containing 3 cwt, or a basket and a half, with the coals hewn down by the getter; and dragging it on its sledge bottom by means of a girdle of leather passing round the body, and a chain of iron attached to that girdle in front, and hooked to the sledge. The sledge has to be dragged to the mainway leading to the shaft, which is run nearly upon a level... 'Thrutchers' are little boys employed to help the weaker drawers by 'thrutching', or thrusting, at the back of the tub or truck.

In this district, to the east of Manchester, it is not the custom to employ females of any age in the pits, partly perhaps because of the employment which is afforded them by the cotton factories which abound throughout its extent. The custom is now so firmly fixed that a man from Wigan, who came to work for Messrs Lees and Jones, went away again because he was not allowed to work his wife in the pit. At no age whatever are girls worked in the pits. Girls as well as women do work in the pits on the other side of Manchester, but if he had the 'ordering of it' there should be no female children whatever so employed. The postures, and the labour, and the intermingling with the men and boys in the dark and illgoverned recesses of the mine, are quite inconsistent with any delicacy of manners or conduct. There is no restraint whatever in a coal-pit from the extremest grossness, of which he adduced instances within his own knowledge. (Signed) Henry Garforth. (*First report.*)

A pit girl from Halifax

Patience Kershaw, aged 17.

My father has been dead about a year; my mother is living and has ten children, five lads and five lasses; the oldest is about thirty, the youngest is four; three lasses go to mill; all the lads are colliers, two getters and three hurriers; one lives at home and does nothing; mother does nought but look after home.

Name	Age	Occupation	Wages £ s d
William Kershaw	22	Getter	0 16 0
Thomas—married			
James	18	Hurrier	0 8 6
Bethel	13	Ditto	0 5 0
Solomon	11	Ditto	0 3 6
Patience	17	Ditto	0 8 6
Sarah	24	Weaver	0 9 0
Hannah	21	Ditto	0 9 0
Sybil—married	26		
Caroline—at home	4		
Alice—at home, sick	15		
			£2 19 6

All my sisters have been hurriers, but three went to the mill, Alice went because her legs swelled from hurrying in cold water when she was hot. I never went to day-school; I go to Sunday-school, but I cannot read or write; I go to pit at five o'clock in the morning and come out at five in the evening; I get my breakfast of porridge and milk first; I take my dinner with me, a cake, and eat it as I go; I do not stop or rest any time for the purpose; I get nothing else until I get home, and then have potatoes and meat, not every day meat. I hurry in the clothes I have now got on, trousers and ragged jacket; the bald place upon my head is made by thrusting the corves; my legs have never swelled, but sisters' did when they went to mill; I hurry the corves a mile and more under ground and back; they weigh 300 cwt; I hurry 11 a-day; I wear a belt and chain at the workings to get the corves out; the getters that I work for are *naked* except their caps; they pull off all their clothes; I see them at work when I go up; sometimes they beat me, if I am not quick enough, with their hands; they strike me upon my back; the boys take liberties with me sometimes, they pull me about; I am the only girl in the pit; there are about 20 boys and 15 men; all the men are naked; I would rather work in mill than in coal-pit.

This girl is an ignorant, filthy, ragged, and deplorable-looking object, and such an one as the uncivilized natives of the prairies would be shocked to look upon. (*First report.*)

Song 23 *The collier lass*

My name's Polly Parker, I come o'er from Worsley. My father and mother work in the coal mine. Our family's large, we have got seven children. So I am obliged to work in the same mine. As this is my fortune, I know you'll feel sorry That in such employment my days I shall pass. I keep up my spirits, I sing and look merry, Although I am but a poor collier lass.

2 By the greatest of dangers each day I'm surrounded;
I hang in the air by a rope or a chain.
The mine may fall in, I may be killed or wounded,
May perish by damp or the fire of the train.
And what would you do if it weren't for our labour?
In wretched starvation your days you would pass,
While we could provide you with life's greatest blessing –
Then do not despise the poor collier lass.

3 Now all the day long you may say we are buried,
Deprived of the light and the warmth of the sun;
And often at nights from our bed we are hurried:
The water is in and then barefoot we run.
And though we go ragged and black are our faces,
As kind and as free as the best we'll be found;
Our hearts are as white as your lords, in fine places,
Although we're poor colliers that work underground.

4 I'm growing up fast, now, one way or another;
There's a collier lad strangely runs in my mind.
In spite of the talking of father and mother,
I think I should marry if he was inclined.
But should he prove surly and would not befriend me,
Another and better chance may come to pass.
My friends here, I know, to him will commend me,
And I'll be no longer a collier lass.

Damp: methane gas, or 'firedamp' is inflammable and, when mixed with air, highly explosive. Alternatively, damp may refer to carbon dioxide, or 'choke-damp' which caused suffocation.

An invitation declined, 1841

I entered several houses, which were miserably furnished, and agreed with the general aspect of the exterior. The first I entered was occupied by a collier and his family, consisting of a wife and six children; the furniture of this house, that is, bed, bedding, chairs, tables, kitchen utensils, &c, if put up to the hammer, might probably have realised 10s. A few days previously to my visit, the father and the eldest son, who worked in the coal-pits, and were the support of the family, had both been seriously burned by an explosion of gas, or as they call it, 'fire-damp' in the pit, and were both disabled. The father expected soon to be able to resume his work, but the son was so dreadfully burned on the face, head, and arms, that it was thought at one time that he would lose his sight; however, when I called, he had hopes that would not be the case; but it was thought he would not be able to work for three months...I had an invitation to go down the pit and examine the place where the explosion occurred; but, thinking this would be incurring unnecessary danger, I declined. (William Dodd, writing from Wigan, 21 October 1841.)

A Norfolk man in Manchester

I found that Child Labour was there [in Manchester] too. You would see little chaps goen with there fathers to the Coal pit, carrien there tin food box and tea can. They went down in the pits at a verry early age and were called Trappers, that is to say they had to sit besides a canvas door, and open it for the skips drawn by the pit ponies to pass through, and then close it after them. The object was to stop the coal dust from getten in the workings, and keep the good air in the lower seams of coal.

On the top you would see plenty of young girls picken Cole. As it was brought to the top it was shot into screens and then the girls picked the pices of slate and rock out as it slid down the screens. That was what was called Hand picked cole; we do not se much of that down this way.

I went down a pit once one afternoon, the first and last time they ever got me down one of them places. It was called Pin Mill pit, belongen to the Clifton and Kersley Company. I was friendly with the Foreman and he fixed it. They gave me a sute of Over Alls, and I got into the cage with the other men with the safty lamp in my hand and my matches and pipe all took away from me. The bell rang and down we went – and a most horrible feeling it is, some thing like Jumping from the top of a high tower or steeple must be, your whole inside seams to lose its moorings and come up inside your throat.

The pit was eight Hundred feet deep, but we seam to be there as soon as we started, perhaps because I would have sooner been some were else. Wen we arived at the botom wich is called the Sump, I with the other Colliers got into one of the small skips and were carried to the face of the Cole, drawen by the pit ponies. The little pit boys were set down as we came to the canvas doors, to set there in the dark for eight hours on end.

Wen we arived at the Cole face I was told I could go up any gallary were I could hear the sound of the pick at work. There was a terrible explosion in this pit the year before I went down, and I believe there were close on one hundred men and boys killed. Every now and then as you went along you could se a name chalked up at diffrent spots I wanted to know what they meant and then they told me that was the place were diffrent men were picked up dead, killed by the After Damp, not very cheerful I did'nt think, but then I had no liken for cole mines.

I staid down till the four hour men came up, and I came up with them and glad I was to get out of it, being fed up with mines and all to do with them. You would think wen you were down there you were in a large wood with the props standing about – thousands of them. You would hear them burst like the crack of a whip, but there were always men there to put in fresh ones at once. There was a continuall drip of water evrywere, and the cole Hewers worked with nothing on except a pair of ragged trousers and Clogs. I know I was whet through and as black as any collier wen I got to the top, resolved never to go down a cole mine again if I knew it.

Of corse I Joined in the Sports of the Colliers and mill workers, and they did a lot in that line up there. I did not care for some such as Rat corsen and Pigeon flying, but I was fond of Whippet racing, and brought out a good Whippet and won a lot of corses with him. There was a place in Ancoats were they used to have Cock fights and Dog fights, but there I never went though I might have done had I liked. I have never been a religus man but I did not care for that sort of sport on a Sunday morning. (The King of the Norfolk Poachers, *I walked by night*, 1939.)

Song 24 *The collier*

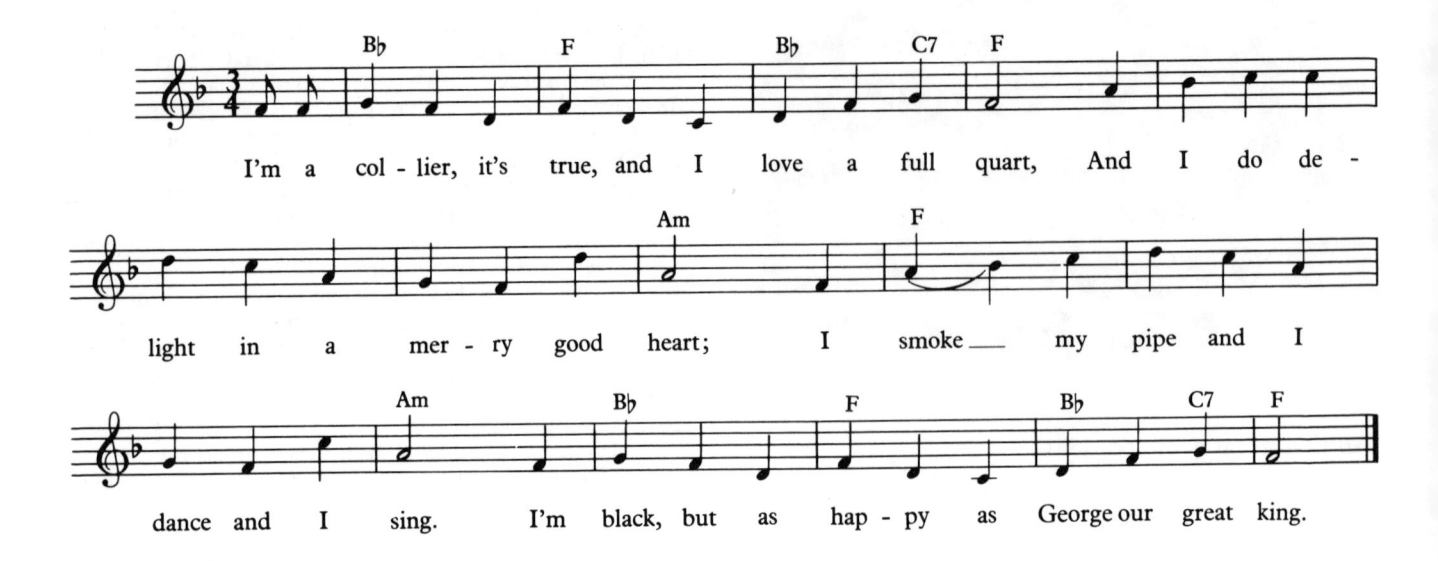

I'm a collier, it's true, and I love a full quart, And I do delight in a merry good heart; I smoke my pipe and I dance and I sing. I'm black, but as happy as George our great king.

2. I'm a lad, to the coal-pit each morning I go,
I ride in the skip to the coal down below,
And with my small pick if I work very well,
Black work gets white money and gold also.

3. I strip coat and waistcoat and shirt off, to work,
And he that's a collier, he must never lurk.
We must get some money for our good wives,
And they shall have tea all the days of their lives.

4. Sometimes I sit cross-legg'd when using my pick,
Which makes the sweat run down when hard I do strike,
Whilst up above me the great coals they do crash,
The pick do strike fire, all around me it flash.

5. In the midst of great dangers we work and we sweat;
The engine above us it draws up the wet.
When Jack says, 'Come up', and when Jemmy says, 'Haul',
The coals shake the earth whenever they fall.

Skip: basket.

The song would appear to date from the late 1820s, for three reasons: the miner rides in a skip, not a cage (and cages did not start to come in until the late 1830s); 'George our great king' was presumably George IV, who died in 1830; the 'engine above us (which) draws up the wet' may well be one of the efficient Boulton and Watt pumping engines which came into widespread use in the first quarter of the nineteenth century.

Miner at work

More evidence on pit life

Samuel Walkden, collier in the employment of Mr Wrigley, at the Low Side Mine, for between 18 and 20 years.–October 29, 1841.

Will be 65 years of age next March, and has been a collier all his life; at first at the Duke of Bridgewater's works at Walkden Moor; has worked at Bolton and in other parts of the county, and has worked up in the neighbourhood of Oldham for 23 years. Two bits of lads working with him have to draw the tubs of 3 cwt each down the 'broo' for 40 yards, dipping about two yards in seven on sleds. In some places, in the same pit, the coal will dip one yard in two; when the lads get the tubs into the main-way, one by one, they load two on a waggon-body, and push that on four wheels on the rails to the pit-bottom. The tubs are sledded down the 40 yards incline by the belt and chain. The two lads working for him will be one 13 years of age next Christmas, the other is going in 15; to the first he is grandfather. The first has been three years in the pit; the other may have been six or seven years in the pit, but he cannot say. Poverty makes the parents bring them in very soon. They bring children down about nine years of age to receive wages at 9*d* or 1*s* a-day. Where there is a great family they will bring them from their cradle, if they can. They bring them to learn a bit at first, and see how the other lads get on; and then they begin thrutching, till they are bald with wearing the hair off their heads. Is himself an old 'fellow' who works at easy places, that yet require judgment to get no more than is required from the pillars without letting them down, and requires two boys to take away his coals. Never knew in this district more than one woman at work, and this was at Squire Greaves's for a week, where he was himself underlooker; but the men said they would leave work if she continued, and so both she and the husband had to go. Gave her 14*s* out of the club to carry her off. But down in Worsley district, under the Duke's (now Lord Francis Egerton's), women work in the pits common enough, and little girls, too, heaving up with a belt and chain. The men send them anywhere for something to eat. When in full work the lads in the pit where he is at work are at it for 12 working hours. The men can come out a bit sooner, an hour or two sometimes. Work regularly double sets, night and day, and have done that for six years and more. The night set goes down about seven, or sometimes nearer eight; and sometimes they are up next morning at seven; sometimes they are up by five; but sometimes not till after seven. The day set go down between seven and eight regularly, and they come up, the men at four or five, but the lads will not until between seven and eight. The night set one week is the day set next week, except that the old men like himself work only in the day set.

The children, when bed-time comes on them, begin to be drowsy and sleepy in the night; and the only way to keep them awake is to give them a good souse on the side of the head, kick their —, or give them a good shake. When the demand has been very busy, the Saturday-night set have worked on until Sunday morning, 'cheating the Lord as they thought'. But generally the men who finish their night shift on Saturday morning go next into the pit as the day shift on Monday morning. But if there is work to be done, it must be done, Sunday or workday. A return of the number of children has been made to the Commission, by the proprietor of the pit in which he works. The master wants them to keep off drinking, pay their way, and follow their work. Are now making only four days a-week, or three and a half in summer-time, and yet are working night shifts and day shifts. Men are now making less than a pound a-week: a full day's work is reckoned 5*s*. His two lads get 3*s* a-day; one having 1*s* 9*d*, and the other 1*s* 3*d*. Sometimes two have 1*s* 3*d* a-piece. Sometimes one has 9*d*, and the other 2*s* 3*d*; all according to their strength. If you ill use a child in our pit, you must take up your tools and be off. The underlooker will allow neither swearing nor fighting. 'Them as is religious would tell the underlooker – ay, by George, sure.' The lads are mostly well done to at home, else they could not follow the work. They seem to be fed as well as the wages will allow.

Is certain parents bring children earlier into the pit than they did, sin' masters began 'bating their wages. Some are sent to the factory first, and then brought into the pit after. Even if the children can merely sit down, and keep the rats from their dinners, they will bring them down. Children cannot see their own danger, but their parents take care of them. (Signed) SAMUEL WALKDEN X his mark (*First report.*)

Song 25 *Five in the morning*

At five in the morning the miner does rise, To go to his dangerous labour; His bottle and bag round his neck he does hang And calls on his next-door neighbour. And calls on his next-door neighbour.

2. With his pick, drill and scraper he goes down the shaft,
With pit lamp so dimly burning,
To the bowels of the earth and the place of his birth,
To wait for the fireman returning.

3. All right, says the fireman; the miner goes in;
He strips off his clothes to his breeches;
The pick he does swing and the miner do sing,
As he shoots the black coal down in pieces.

4. At seven in the morning the work they begin;
The miners are soon in full working:
Some picking, some drilling, some blasting the rocks,
And others the waggons are filling.

5. The jig flies with speed away down the steep road,
The horse to the shaft it will take them.
They are put in the cage and then with a loud knock
A lift with the engine will take them.

6. Then look to the danger the miner is in,
As he hangs in the air night and morning;
The rope it may break, he in pieces be dashed,
And his wife left at home she will mourn him.

7. An accident sometimes takes place from the gas,
And gives the poor miner no warning;
A fall from the roof can likewise cause his death,
Leave fatherless children grieving.

8. Come all you coal miners who hear these few lines,
Come look to the old and the feeble;
The wife and the children will surely want bread,
To work you know they are not able.

Fireman: person who used to check pits for gas and, in some cases, fire pockets of it.
Jig: device by which a series of loaded waggons running downhill pulled empty ones uphill by means of a cable which ran round a wheel.

From pitman to hewer

In the 'olden time' [late eighteenth century,] the early years of a pitman's life – that is, from the time of taking his 'seat' behind the 'door' until he took up the 'picks' to 'hew' – or, in other words, from his being a 'trapper' at six years of age until he became a 'hewer' at about twenty – were nearly all spent 'belaw', with frequently only very short intervals for rest.

The youthful portion of a pitman's life in those days was passed in the most galling slavery – eighteen or nineteen hours a day, for weeks together, being spent in almost insupportable drudgery. The putters of the present day would not be able to comprehend how such incessant toil could be endured...The application of gun-powder has also been a great improvement in the labour of 'hewing'.

At the age of twenty, when a 'pitman' became a 'hewer', his labour, though still severe, was very much shortened. Instead of being sixteen or eighteen hours, his drudgery was reduced to eight or ten. He then got time to look around him in daylight, and form such connections as made the 'weal or woe' of his future life. In short, he soon got married. (Thomas Wilson, *The pitman's pay*, 1843, preface.)

From pony-putting I went to coal-hewing before I was quite eighteen years of age [1855]. The demand for putters was much greater than the demand for hewers, so that the transition from the one job to the other was not without difficulty. I was eager to hew. The work was much harder, but the hours were shorter and the pay was higher.

I had now, so to speak, completed my apprenticeship. I had passed through all the common stages of pit life, from trapper-boy to coal hewer. So far as my work was concerned, I now ceased to be a boy, and henceforth was a man. As a coal-hewer there were yet ten more years of underground life before me. Roughly speaking, half of that time was to be spent at Seaton Delaval and the other half at Choppington Colliery. These were years of hard work and moderate pay. They were, on the whole, very pleasant years, some of the happiest of a not unhappy life.

The hewer is paid by the ton. His earnings, therefore, depend partly upon his industry, strength, and skill, and partly upon his luck. To give an equal chance to everybody, the places were 'cavilled', or balloted for, once a quarter. The hewers grouped themselves into parties of four, these 'marrows' working together, two in each shift, and dividing the total earnings among them on the pay Friday, which came once a fortnight.

The hours of hewers at Delaval then [1855-60] were about eight hours from bank to bank. The wage would run about 5s a day. That was then deemed a good wage, and I think it would be above the average of the county. During the winter months work was irregular. Taking the year round, the pots would probably work about nine days a fortnight. The miner then nearly always had his house and coal free, a small sum of sixpence a fortnight being charged for the carting of the fuel. After making deductions for powder, candles and working tools, and for the irregularity of employment, the hewer's wage at this period would probably average, the year round, from 21s to 23s per week. (Thomas Burt, *Autobiography*.)

Miner with a safety lamp

Song 26 *The collier lads*

Attend awhile, you workmen, wherever you may be, I pray you give attention and listen unto me: Concerning the poor collier lads, their equal ne'er was found, For all the trades they do depend on the lads that are underground.

2   In olden times the farmers used themselves to plough and sow:
    It was their glory and their pride to hold the painful plough;
    While Johnny led the team along, he'd sing with joyful sound,
    Not thinking of the sufferings of the lads that are underground.

3   The plough's not made without the fire, nor fire without the coal.
    D'you see what is depending on a collier lad, poor soul?
    You may search the wide world over, their equal is not found;
    We cannot do without the lads that labour underground.

4   The mariner where'er he steers across the raging sea,
    Mechanics, too, and artisans, with their machinery,
    Have all to thank the collier lad, whom danger does surround,
    So ne'er despise the collier lads that labour underground.

5   Cold winter is approaching, the morn looks dark and drear,
    To see a collier take farewell of his wife and children dear;
    For when he does descend the shaft and to his work goes down,
    He never may return alive from his labour underground.

6   It's but a few short weeks ago, most shocking for to hear,
    That some poor lads they met their death at Cannock, Staffordshire,*
    The widows and orphans were relieved by gentlemen round,
    Who know the worth of the collier lads that labour underground.

7   All trades they would be standing, it's plainly to be seen,
    We cannot do without them, from the beggar to the Queen.
    If you were to ask the gentlemen where they get their thousand pounds,
    They'd say 'twas by the collier lads that labour underground.

8 So to conclude my ditty, be merry and be wise,
And from this time a collier lad you never must despise;
His health drink in a bumper and let the toast go round:
Success to all the collier lads that labour underground.

* The place is left blank in the original.

Working in a Black Country pit

Marriage

Shortly after settling at Choppington [Northumberland, in 1860], I married my cousin, Mary Weatherburn. Never was wedding quieter or less demonstrative. The marriage ceremony took place at Bedlington, about two miles from Choppington. On a cold, bright winter morning the youthful bride and bridegroom walked through the Netherton fields to the old church, where they were met by my father. The three of us, with the officiating clergyman, were the only persons present. Whether in going or in returning, or at the church, happily nobody took the slightest notice of us. Next day I went to my coalhewing as though nothing unusual had happened. And yet the event was one of the most momentous of my life. Beyond doubt this was the best day's work I had ever done, or was likely to do. (Thomas Burt, *Autobiography*.)

The strike in South Wales – colliers 'stepping', February 1873

Song 27 *Down among the coal*

You men of wealth and lux-u-ry in coun-ty, town or shire, You sel-dom give a thought to us while sit-ting by your fire, Or think up-on the dan-gers that threat-en each poor soul, As fear-less-ly they go to work to hew and dig the coal. Down a-mong the coal, lads, down a-mong the coal, All a-lone and in the dark, I tell you it's no lark; Down a-mong the coal, my lads, oh, down a-mong the coal, And it's hard work the life of a mi-ner un-der-ground.

2. Down shafts ill-ventilated the miner he must go
   And crawl upon his hands and knees whene'er the roof is low;
   The hewer, putter, driver and the trapper in his hole,
   Are all exposed to danger whilst down among the coal.

3. Without the collier, England would not gain half her fame;
   Without the collier, doubtless, we never would had steam;
   Without old Geordie Stephenson, no steam engine would roll,
   For Geordie was a collier, too, and worked among the coal.

4. While in the dark and dreary mine, begrimed with dust and sweat,
   While thinking on sweethearts and wives and some dear household pet,
   'The pit's on fire', that dreadful word sends terror to each soul;
   Overcome by gas, the miner meets his death among the coal.

5. So just bestow a thought on us that labour down below,
   That work so hard by day and night to make your fireside glow,
   There is no harder working men, if you search from pole to pole,
   Than the honest-hearted miner who hews and digs the coal.

Song 28 *Lament for John Sneddon*

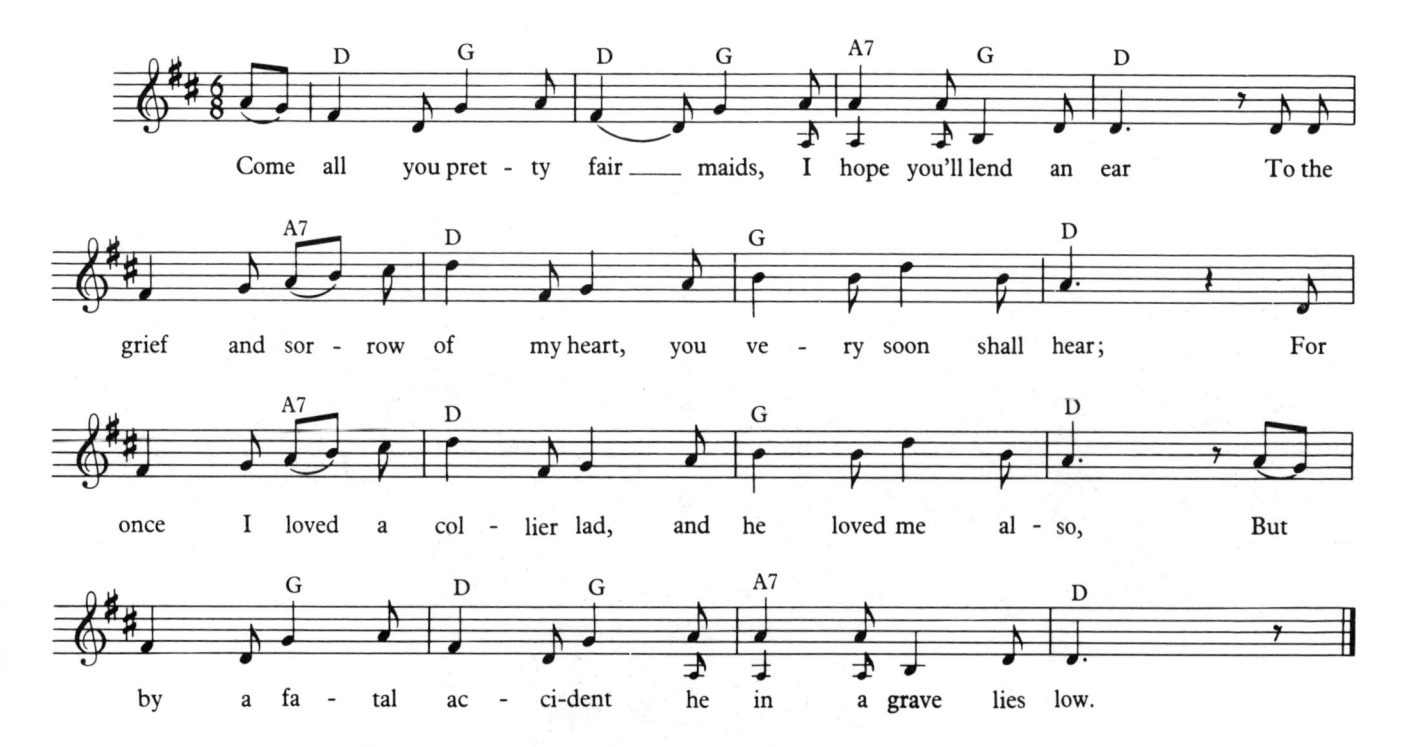

Come all you pretty fair maids, I hope you'll lend an ear
To the grief and sorrow of my heart, you very soon shall hear;
For once I loved a collier lad, and he loved me also,
But by a fatal accident he in a grave lies low.

2 My love he was a collier lad, he wrought beneath the ground;
   For mild and good behaviour, his equal can't be found,
   He'd light blue eyes and yellow hair and cheeks like roses red,
   But now my handsome collier lad lies numbered with the dead.

3 The night my true-love he was killed, as I lay on my bed,
   I dreamt my love appeared to me and thus to me he said:
   'Farewell, my dearest Jennie, for me you need not mourn;
   My spirit's fled, I'm with the dead, I'll never more return'.

4 Early the next morning, my dream was verified;
   The neighbours all came rushing in, 'John Sneddon's killed', they cried;
   'As he was at his work last night the roof all on him fell'.
   The grief and sorrow of my heart no mortal tongue can tell.

5 The banns were out, the day was set that married we should be;
   My love and I we had agreed to sail to America,
   In hopes to make a fortune all on that fertile shore,
   But, alas, my dearest collier lad I'll never see no more.

6 The summer will return again and nature will be gay;
   The small birds they will sweetly sing and lambs will sport and play.
   While other maids will happy be, till death I'll constant mourn,
   For the sake of my dear collier lad who'll never more return.

The Gresford disaster, September 1934

The Cannock disaster

One of the greatest colliery disasters, in which several local people lost their lives, took place in Cannock in the 1860's, the explosion taking place as the day and night shifts were changing over; 660 lost their lives and a list of all the victims hung in my grandmother's home for many years. In another pit accident, at Nine Locks, Quarry Bank, miners were entombed for a long period; it is rumoured that they had eaten the pit ponies and harness and had reached the decision of cannibalism. Lots were drawn for the first victim and it fell on a young boy. The hardened old colliers could not carry their plan through. Later they were rescued and the day boy was often pointed out to people as 'the boy that should have been eaten'. (J. Wilson Jones, *The history of the Black Country*.)

An accident at Chasetown (near Cannock)

Now when I was a lad I knew an old chap named Gammy White'us [Whitehouse]. Now Gammy – 'e was called Gammy because 'e'd got one leg shorter than the other and 'e used to go up and down. 'Is pal 'ad also got one leg shorter than the other and it was very funny when they used to go out together to the pubs: as one went up the other'd be going down. And Gammy, who was a bitter wit, 'e used to say to 'is mate, "We'm seen some ups and downs in our time, ae [haven't] we?"

But anyway, the story about Gammy. This is very true – it goes back now to the 1840s. They were buried in the Fly Pit at Chasetown and the horse, Nobby – most of the pit ponies were called Nobby – the Nobby of the time was buried with them. Well, they were there three days in pitch darkness, and there's always one man takes command – 'e will always rise. And the man who rose was Gammy.

Now after three days the food 'ad gone. There was a drop of water, by the way, a little seepage, though relatively fresh water. But 'ow they survived was this. They killed Nobby and ate part of Nobby's stomach, which was the tenderest part, and they survived. They were buried for fourteen days altogether. That was Gammy.

Now another good story about the mines is the man who was buried with 'is two pals; and again, *one* always rises to the top. And this was the man who rose to the top. And 'e said a prayer for all three of 'em. And this was 'is prayer: 'e says, "Lord, if thou'll only get we out of this lot, we woh [won't] bother yo agen for a bloody long while". A man who can joke with 'is maker like that, 'e's a hero. Now that is perfectly true. (Tom Langley, interview with Roy Palmer, 1971.)

Pit accidents, 1868

In the year 1864 the total number of lives lost from different causes in the British collieries and ironstone-mines of the Coal Measures appears, from the official reports, to have been 963, showing a decrease compared with the numbers for 1863 and previous years.

In Great Britain, as also in France, the greatest number of accidents are occasioned by falls of the roof and coal, nearly one-half; then a third take place in the shafts, from breakage of engines, ropes or chains, upsetting or fouling of skips, boxes, tubs, &c. The remaining number, or one-sixth of the casualties, occur from blasting, explosions of fire-damp, suffocation – caused by defective ventilation, or for want of air, or by poisonous gases, carbonic acid and after-damp – and, finally, inundations. It is true, then, that a piece of coal often costs more than is supposed, and that the mine is to the collier a real field of battle.

The total quantity of coal raised from 3192 mines by 320,663 miners being 101,630,544 tons, and the proportion of deaths having been about one in every 216 persons employed in 1866, according to the last Annual Report of Her Majesty's Inspectors of Mines, the result is that on an average one accident takes place for every 147,925·5 tons of coal raised, and one life is lost for every 68,484 tons. Even in the Derby, Nottingham, Leicester, and Warwickshire coal-fields, the most favoured districts in England, one man is killed for every 131,034 tons of coal raised, while in Yorkshire the proportion is no less than one in 22,235 tons. In West Lancashire and North Wales it is one in 55,666, and in South Wales one in 78,137; but the credit of minimum destructiveness belongs to Scotland, in the western district of which 131,880 tons are raised for every life lost, while in the eastern part of that country the proportion is only one to 190,625 tons.

In the year 1866, 651 lives were lost from explosions of fire-damp, as against 168 in 1865, giving the enormous increase of 483 out of the gross increase for the year from all causes, which is exactly 500. The number of lives lost in the inspected ironstone-mines of Great Britain in 1866 amounted to 81. Taking the several groups of Inspectors' districts into which the coal-fields of the country are divided, the returns show the following results for each of the years 1865 and 1866 respectively: To one death, the number of miners employed was 636 and 83 in Yorkshire; 403 and 112 in North Stafford, Chester, and Salop; 238 and 200 in West Lancaster and North Wales; 182 and 243 in South Wales; 296 and 248 in South Stafford and Worcester; 258 and 259 in Northumberland, Cumberland, and North Durham; 414 and 310 in South Durham; 325 and 321 in Monmouth, Gloucester, Somerset, and Devon; 356 and 368 in North and East Lancaster; 330 and 467 in Derby, Nottingham, Leicester, and Warwick; 340 and 445 in the western districts of Scotland; and 450 and 662 in the eastern districts of Scotland. Out of the 1484 deaths in 1866, 651 occurred from explosions of fire-damp. The deaths from this cause alone in Great Britain in the ten years 1856 to 1865 were 2019. The total number of deaths from all violent causes in the ten years was 9916, about twenty per cent. of which was caused by fire-damp explosions. The number of deaths from falls in mines in 1866 was 361; from accidents in shafts, 162; from accidents underground, 203; and from accidents on the surface, 107. Of the deaths from fire-damp, 361 occurred in the Oaks Colliery, 91 at Talk-o'-th'-Hill Colliery, and 38 in the Victoria Colliery in Dukinfield.

Right: Rescue workers leaving Gresford pithead

The following list will convey an idea of the terrific nature of the explosions of fire-damp in the English mines:

Year	Men perished
1812 at Felen's Colliery	92
1835 at Wallsend Colliery	102
1844 at Haswell Colliery	95
1856 at Cymmer, Rhonddu Colliery	114
1857 at Lundhill Colliery	189
1860 at Risca Colliery	142
1866 at Oaks Colliery	361
1866 at Talk-o'-th'-Hill Colliery	91

From the Oaks Colliery they are only now (October, 1867) beginning the terrible task of recovering the bodies of the dead. Of the accidents in which less than ninety were killed, no notice has been taken in this list.

The proportion of accidents and lives lost to the number of persons employed, and the tons of coal raised, in 1866

The number of accidents involving loss of life in the collieries of the United Kingdom are	837
The number of lives lost by those accidents are	1484
The number of collieries in the United Kingdom are	3192
The present quantity of coal raised	101,630,544 tons
A life is lost for every of coal raised	68,484 tons
Tons of coal raised per separate fatal accident	117,537
Persons employed per separate fatal accident	374
Persons employed per life lost	216
The number of coal-miners in Great Britain	320,663

The accidents, when analyzed, are annually as follows:

By explosion of fire-damp	169·6
By falls of roof	446·6
By falls, &c, in shafts	197·0
By sundry causes	196·1
	1009·3

(L. Simonin, *Mines and miners*, 1868.)

Song 29 *The Gresford disaster*

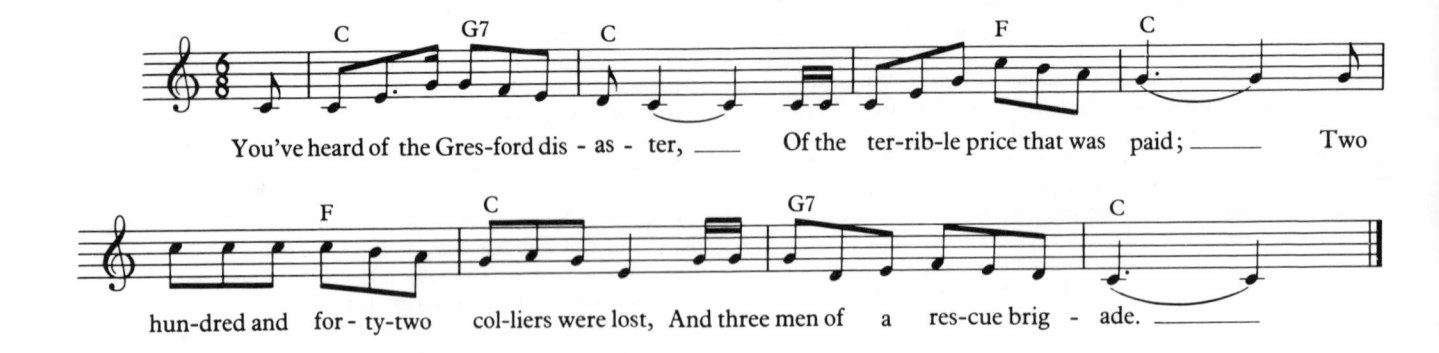

You've heard of the Gresford disaster, Of the terrible price that was paid; Two hundred and forty-two colliers were lost, And three men of a rescue brigade.

2. It occurred in the month of September;
   At three in the morning the pit
   Was racked by a violent explosion
   In the Dennis where gas lay so thick.

3. Now the gas in the Dennis deep section
   Was heaped there like snow in a drift,
   And many a man had to leave the coal-face
   Before he had worked out his shift.

4. Now a fortnight before the explosion,
   To the shotfirer Tomlinson cried,
   'If you fire that shot we'll be all blown to hell',
   And no one can say that he lied.

5. Now the fireman's reports they are missing,
   The records of forty-two days;
   The collier manager had them destroyed,
   To cover his criminal ways.

6. Down there in the dark they are lying,
   They died for nine shillings a day.
   They have worked out their shift and now they must lie
   In the darkness until Judgement Day.

7. Now the Lord Mayor of London's collecting,
   To help out our children and wives;
   The owners have sent some white lilies
   To pay for the poor colliers' lives.

8. Farewell all our dear wives and children,
   Farewell all our comrades as well;
   Don't send your sons down the dark dreary pit,
   They'll be doomed like the sinners in hell.

The Gresford disaster occurred on Friday 22 September 1934. In fact, 265 miners were killed, including three rescue men. Gresford is in Denbighshire, near Wrexham. A commemorative service is still held there every year. The Gresford Colliery was finally closed in November, 1973.

Ambulance men standing by at the Gresford Colliery, 24 September 1934

The Gresford Colliery disaster: accounts by three eye-witnesses

1. Mr Charles H. Jones

I was one of the miners working down the disaster mine when it happened about 2.0 a.m. I also went down the disaster area on the Sat. night to help with the rescue teams. It was a terrible mess. I have been a miner from leaving school at 14 yrs old till I retired in 1968 after completing 51 yrs service in the mine. Out of the 51 yrs I worked 36 yrs nights regular. Now back to the disaster. My one and only best pal went under with his father and I will say this, I haven't had a pal like him since. Only those who work in a mine knows how those men died.

2. Mr G. K. Tilston

I was first called out to the Colliery at 2.30 a.m. on Saturday 22nd September 1934. When I arrived the Senior Overman and I decided to go down the pit immediately and not wait the arrival of the other rescue men.

Everything appeared normal at the pit bottom so we proceeded to the Main Dennis District where it was thought that the explosion had occurred. We made our way through many falls of roof and after going about ½ mile we met six men making their way to the pit bottom. They had only one lamp between them and were in a distressed state, evidently suffering from the effects of gas. We were told that they had left approximately 70 men in 29 District which was on a lower level known as the ladder, these men having decided to stay put until help arrived.

We made our way in the direction of the ladder but after going some way it was noticed that the canary* I was carrying was dead and that we could not go any further along that particular roadway.

Retracing our steps, we thought it might be possible to reach these 70 men from another direction, i.e. down the Dennis Deep. At what is known as 29 Turn we were met by fire, everything that would burn being alight, including pit props and tubs of coal, the whole scene being one of destruction. At this stage we were joined by other men and tried to fight the fire for about two hours, but the equipment we had was inadequate.

Word reached us eventually that rescue men were in difficulties in another district and we proceeded to the spot. Five men were involved but two had managed to escape. We found two bodies which were brought out but failed to reach the other man at that time. (His body was recovered after the pit was re-opened.)

My first break was mid-day on Saturday and I was called out again that evening at 6.0 p.m. to assist fighting the fire which was spreading rapidly towards the pit bottom. The maximum time we were allowed to do this without a break was 2 hrs and we continued doing this work until the Sunday evening at 6.0 p.m. the Chief Inspector of Mines considered the position had become too dangerous.

All men were called out and both pits were sealed off at the pit top. On Monday the stopping at the top of the Dennis Shaft exploded, killing a man working approximately 30 yards from the scene. The pit was re-sealed but the following day the fan drift exploded, throwing debris as far as the main Chester Rd.

With a view to re-opening the pit at some future time, work was started to build an air lock at the top of the Martin Shaft, this work taking a few months to complete.

We made the first exploratory descent in early March 1935 and once it was considered safe we started to build stoppings around the pit bottom so that this area could be cleared of gas.

Once this had been accomplished we were able to proceed in-bye.** This was done by building stoppings, clearing the area and then continuing to do this step by step until the work was completed.

The section where the explosions occurred was left sealed permanently.

3. Mr R. E. Edwards

At the age of 14, I left school and had for the first time in my life to search for work for myself. Times were bad. No one wanted anyone. I travelled around without luck, until finally it was the pits. I started at a very old colliery, over 100 years old: the Vron Colliery, a part company of the Broughtons Plas Power Company. At the age of 15 I had the chance of starting in the fitting shop. My boss, Robert Jones, was a very clever man. He had worked at the Brymbo Steelworks, and also in Canada. His wages for a full week would be about 30s to 36s and mine 1s odd a day. Fitters and electricians worked together in the same shop. Chargehand fitter Robert Jones, fitter Robert Roberts and myself, an apprentice; chargehand electrician William Williams, electricians Bryn Edwards and Ern Harrison, what a happy lot we were. Tom Jones was the manager, and Isaac Jones the under manager. This colliery closed down in late 1927, and I was sent to Gresford, and started once again with the fitters underground. George Holmes was my boss, and the fitters included Tom Hughes, Don Slade and shaft fitters Tom Tilston and Sam Roberts, and pipe fitter D. Owens.

In the late 1929s to 30s, things looked bad. Three days a week – dole. Jobs were hard to find, but I was one of the lucky ones. I did not miss much. I have seen the time when all stood outside the office waiting to be picked for a job. When one had been chosen, the others went home, waiting to hear the hooter the next day if there was any work for them. Days passed, and still the same short time, and I firmly believe that this could have been the start of the Gresford disaster. You see, the pit work is, when coal is drawn off the coal face, something has to be replaced to support the roof and make roadways. If there were no roadways, well, there would be no ventilation. As time went on, Districts were going further in; that meant roadways and airways. Things were bad, jobs hard to find, and everyone in the pit had to scrape for a living. The colliers' rate was about 7s 9d a shift and the fillers (men who loaded the tubs) about 6s a shift. My wages were around 3s to 4s a day. I started work at 6.0 a.m., and very often reached home at 9.0 p.m., walking about 8 miles when breakdowns happened.

Up to the tragic night of September 1934, everyone who worked in the pit had the feeling that sometime, something serious was going to happen. The conditions down the pit, and the heat on working coal faces was unbearable. But we all had our jobs to do, and no one seemed to grumble: they just accepted it as normal conditions. In the enquiry of the disaster, all the fault lay at 14's face. I was young then, only in my 20s. I had travelled underground in many Districts, and I believe it could have happened anywhere in the pit any time, but it just happened in the Dennis District. There was the Dennis District, about two to three miles from pit bottom, and No.1 North, which had three to four Districts, and Brassy District. By District, I mean coal faces, some four

---

* Canaries were sometimes taken down the pit as a test for the presence of gas.

** Into the workings, away from the pit bottom.

Districts, 100 yards long, and some larger. Then the low seams, 13's and 14's Brassy, but on the point of closing down. Most of the colliers off 13's and 14's were sent to 14's Dennis, which was a new District opened out.

It was in the Dennis District that the disaster happened. I lived with my parents at Lodge, Brymbo, and travelled on my bike to work on the Saturday morning. On the way, I met people on the road who were shouting, 'Gresford's blown up'. I took no notice of them, but carried on to work. When I got to the works yard, it was alive with people. I went to see my boss George Holmes, and I heard the call for volunteers, so off I went for my lamp, and went down the pit. What a sight. I was asked if I would take sand to put out the fire. So I took a horse and wagon down to the clutch, about halfway from pit bottom, and took two loads. There was no roadway, only the tops of the falling roof made over the old girders and rails placed on top. When I came up from the clutch the second time, my boss told me to get a pipeline main coupled up from pit bottom to top of the Dennis. This I did, and at 12.0 a.m., my boss told me I had better go home and let my parents know that I was all right, and he asked me if I would come in on Sunday morning. I came in on the 6.0 a.m. to 2.30 p.m. shift, and when I came up the shaft I was met by pressmen, but I could not tell them anything. It was terrible; people asked me if I had seen their sons and husbands. Then the Salvation Army Band played *O God our help*. It was the worst experience I have ever had. I went home and told my grandfather, an ex-coal miner, all that had happened, and then word came through that they were sealing the pit up. My grandfather told me it would blow up again, and so it did. It blew up the fan-drift on surface, and killed one man.

1938 was the next time I entered the pit. What a difference – new roadways and airways, districts cooler and everyone happy. I left the pit in the late 50s, and never will I go into the pit to work again, I know things have changed. (Letters to Roy Palmer, 1972.)

Song 30 *The brave Dudley boys*

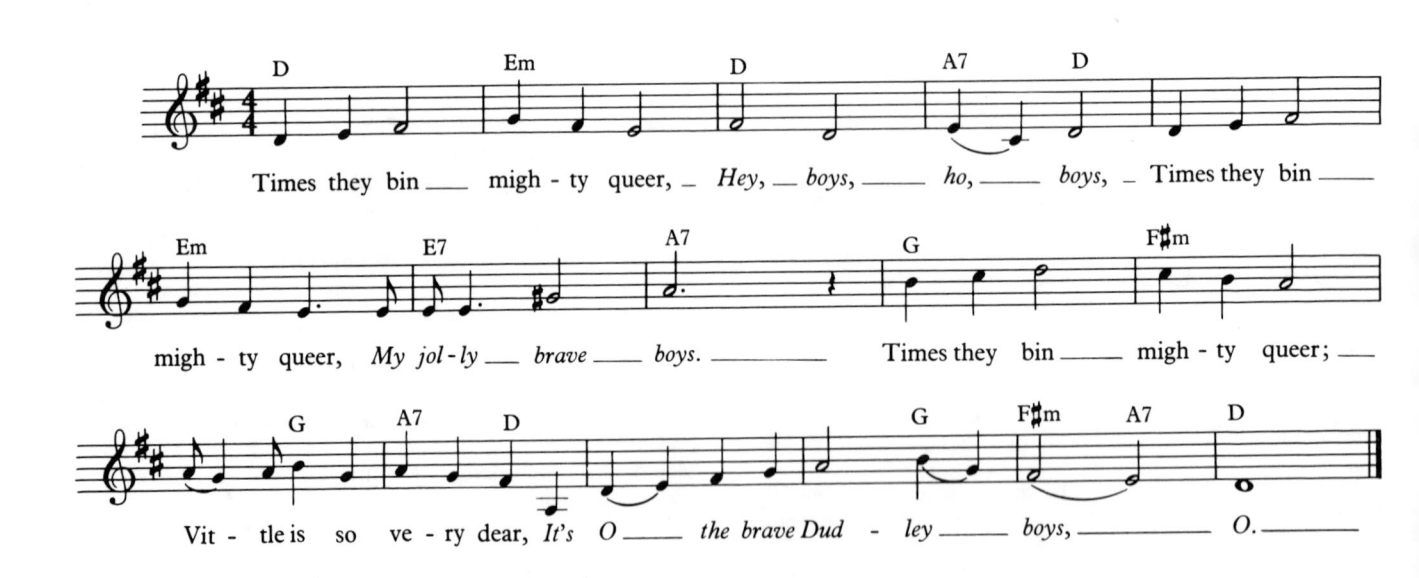

Times they bin mighty queer, Hey, boys, ho, boys, Times they bin mighty queer, My jolly brave boys. Times they bin mighty queer; Vittle is so very dear, It's O the brave Dudley boys, O.

2 We bin marchin' up and down,
 All for to pull the housen down.

3 Some got sticks, some got staves,
 For to beat all the rogues and knaves.

4 Then to make vittle cheap,
 We takes and burns it all of a heap.

5 But dragoons they did come,
 Devil should take the hindmost wum.

6 We all run down our pits,
 For we bin fritten out of we wits.

7 God bless Lord Dudley Ward,
 For he knows these times bin hard.

8 He sent back sojering men,
 We'n promised never to riot again.

Dudley: in Worcestershire. Lord Dudley Ward: probably John, who held the title from 1763 to 1788. Vittle: victuals (food). Wum: home. We wits: our wits.
The song probably dates from the 1790s.

Turbulent colliers

The turbulence of the colliers [in the eighteenth century] is, of course, to be accounted for by something more elementary than politics; it was the instinctive reaction of virility to hunger. Life underground had bred in them a contempt of danger, and if they held their own lives cheap they were hardly likely to set an exaggerated value on those of others. Moreover, the conditions of their daily work imposed on them a discipline and co-operation that could hardly be looked for in the weavers and frame-work knitters of domestic industry. When they set out for bread they marched under captains (possibly their overmen or charter-masters) and when they were forced to retire they found in the pits themselves places of refuge from their pursuers.

Furthermore, the provocation was probably greater in the colliery areas than elsewhere, for the means of distributing foodstuffs were undeveloped, and it was only with difficulty that temporary shortages could be made good. The paucity of dealers and shopkeepers in mining villages was a matter of comment as late as the middle of the nineteenth century: it was at once a cause and a consequence of the prevalence of the truck system. And it meant that when the granaries of Bristol failed to supply the Kingswood colliers, or those of Coventry the miners of Warwickshire, there was no one to explain the true reason, there was no middle-class opinion to sober the counsels of hungry men.

In the riots of the early part of the century the colliers generally remained on good terms with their employers and neighbours. . . .in 1756. . .the colliers who had been arrested in the riots at Nottingham sought shelter behind the name of their employer, the great coal-owner Lord Middleton.

In the later part of the century a more modern tone appears in the demonstrations. Demands are made not only on the corn-factors for lower prices, but also on the employers for higher wages. . .(T. S. Ashton and J. Sykes, *The coal industry of the eighteenth century*, 1929.)

Song 31   *O bury the blackleg*

O bury now the blackleg____ nine feet below the dirt,____ And pile up plenty on him____ of pick and shov-el dirt;____ And heap the stones up-on him,____ put all these un-der seal,____ For fear the dev-il ri-ses to plague the world to come.____

O claddwch y blaclegwr naw troddfedd dan y baw,
A roddwch arno'n helaeth o ffrwyth y gaib a'r rhaw;
A roddwch arno feini a'r rheini oll dan sêl,
Rhag ogn i'r jawl gyfodi i boeni'r oes a ddêl.

Song 32 *The collier lad's lament*

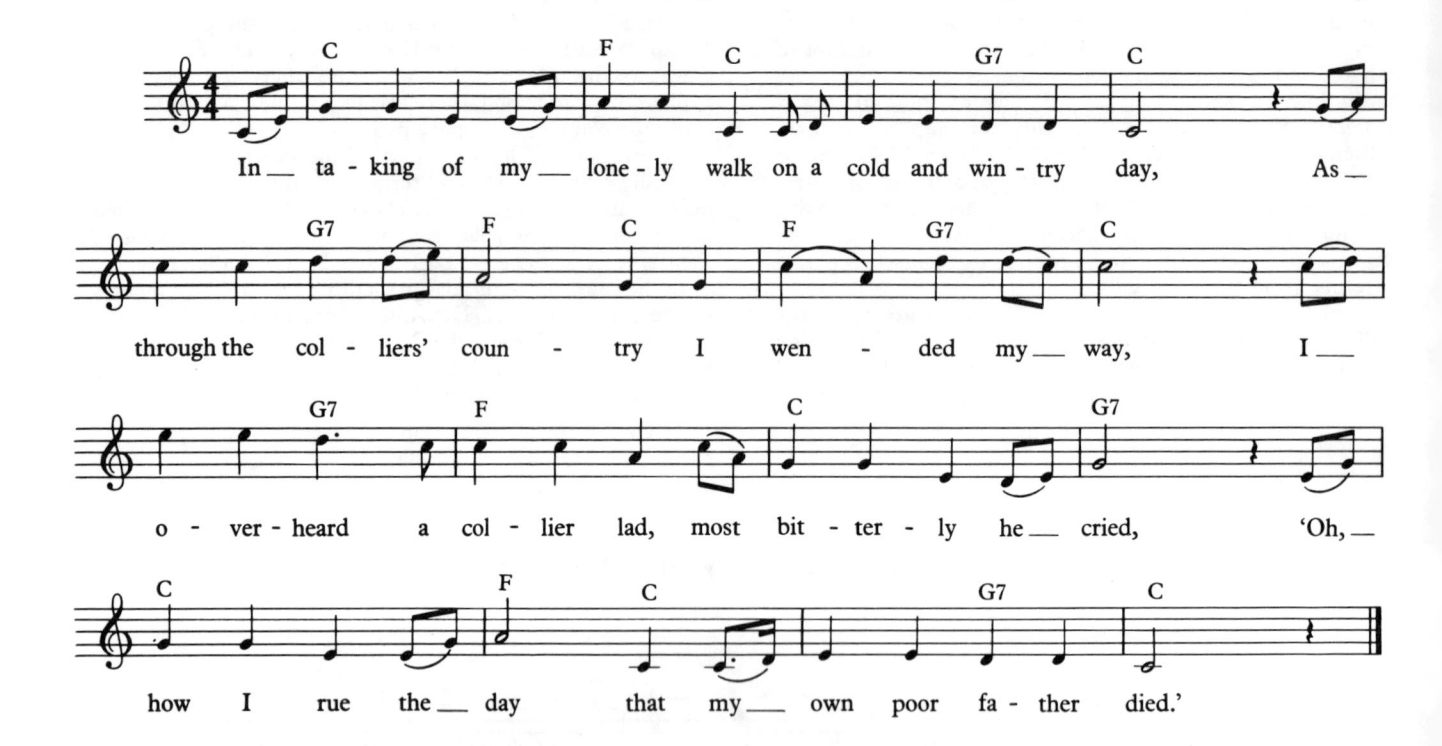

In taking of my lonely walk on a cold and wintry day,
As through the colliers' country I wended my way,
I overheard a collier lad, most bitterly he cried,
'Oh, how I rue the day that my own poor father died.'

2 'When my father he was living, no tommy shops were there;
He did receive good wages and all things went on fair;
And when on Saturday he came home, he to my mother said:
"Come, let us go up into the town to buy our children bread".

3 'To the tommy shop now they're forced to go for all that they do eat,
They're forced to take their wages out in bread and cheese and meat;
And when on Saturday they go to get their wages paid,
The master says, "Do not forget the tommy shop today".

4 'Five and sixpence for a good day's work, it was a collier's due,
But now he thinks hinself well off if he gets more than two;
And if he grumbles at the price, the master thus will say:
"To the workhouse with your children, and there get better pay".

5 'Myself and my poor brother, in the morning we do go
To work upon the coal-pit bank all in the frost and snow;
The little that we both do earn is needless for to tell,
It'll scarcely serve the one of us, the masters pay so well.

6 'But when I do grow up a man, if they don't give better pay,
I'll go and be a soldier for thirteen pence a day,
Before I'll work in those dark pits, with others for to share
The benefit of what I earn in tommy shops and beer.

7 'If the queen and all her ministers, they all were for to come,
To live as these poor colliers do, and work down underground,
And undergo the hardships and dangers of the fire,
I think they'd make the masters pay them better for their hire.

8   'If Johnny Russell he was here and worked upon the bank,
    And Albert he was doggy, for he's of higher rank,
    I think one week would settle them and cause them thus to say:
    "Let these poor colliers have their rights, and give them better pay".'

Tommy shops: tommy or truck was originally payment in goods instead of cash, a practice which was officially made illegal in collieries as early as 1817. Later, straightforward truck was replaced by part-payment in credit notes, which could only be used at particular shops. This practice was also made illegal, but nevertheless persisted well into the second half of the nineteenth century.
The queen: Victoria, who reigned from 1837 until 1901.
Johnny Russell: Lord John Russell (1792-1878), who occupied many different ministries. He was Prime Minister from 1846 to 1852 and Foreign Secretary from 1859 to 1865.
Albert: Prince Albert (1819-61), who was Prince Consort and married to Queen Victoria from 1840 until his death.
Doggy: overman.

It seems safe to argue from the references in the last verse that this ballad appeared during the life-time of Prince Albert and also while Lord John Russell occupied an important ministry. The years between 1846 and 1852 seem to be indicated.

It's his father you are carrying

I especially remember one beautiful September afternoon... [After school] I was away like a whippet, hurtling to the bottom of the Cwm Hill as fast as my little legs would carry me, there to begin the steep ascent up the village's High Street which led to my home. As I neared the terrace in which I lived, I began to hear the distant steady beat of footsteps. This was made by the miners with their heavy hob-nailed working boots as they walked home from the pits. Loud and rhythmic was their tread this time and I realised that some kind of procession was coming along. This made me hurry still more so that I was just in time to see the vanguard rounding the corner some distance away, a formation of miners two abreast. Instantly I realised they were carrying a fellow worker home from the colliery on a stretcher, for at given intervals four miners stepped out to take their turn at sharing the burden of carrying the load...

How grim and determined the miners looked in these processions on such tragic occasions! With worm-like, visible sweat marks on their faces – effects of the daily toil of their job – they looked like black warriors marching relentlessly forward to battle with an unseen foe who always lurked around, ready to pounce at any time, to do them injury or rob them of their lives. Day in, day out, these dusky sons of toil battled in most trying conditions deep in the bowels of the earth, not at all resembling the miners of today in physical appearance...

Years ago each miner wore a dark cloth cap..., a flannel shirt, a knotted red muffler around the neck, a leather belt, and moleskin trousers tightly yorked below the knees (to prevent the dust getting into the eyes!), and hob-nailed boots, not forgetting his glistening 'tommy' box and water jack, and his English lever watch enclosed in a bulbous brass watch-case that bulged out of his waistcoat pocket...The miner's working clothes, often patched, would be as black as his face. The majority of miners on returning home, washed in wooden tubs before the kitchen fire. How alike were these sons of toil! They almost had the stamp of common identity impressed upon them, and as they walked home in one black mass they resembled an 'army strong' marching together from their underworld.

On that memorable September afternoon in 1911, the returning miners marched in solemn procession, beating a kind of rhythmic time as they walked along in their hob-nailed boots, as tom-toms preceding a human sacrifice. Some of my own friends rushed forward as the contingent drew nearer to see which victim it was that the mine had claimed this time. We boys were ordered away by the stretcher-bearers, but my friends shouted and pointed to me. 'Let him stay. It's his father you are carrying.' (Walter Haydn Davies, *The right place, the right time,* 1972.)

Bradley mine near Bilston Staffs

Suggestions for further activities

Records

1. Recordings of songs (not necessarily in the same version) in this book:

No. 2, on *The fine old Yorkshire gentleman* (Folk Heritage Recordings FHR038).

No. 6, on *Roy Bailey* (Leader LER3021), *A dalesman's litany* (Leader LER2029) and *The bitter and the sweet* (Topic 12TS217).

No. 7, on *The iron muse* (Topic Records 12T86) and *Songs, ballads and instrumental tunes from Ulster* (Topic 12TS209).

No. 14, on *The wide Midlands* (Topic 12TS210).

No. 22, on *The fine old Yorkshire gentleman* (see above).

No. 29, on *Steam whistle ballads* (Topic 12T104), *The iron muse* (see above) and *Jack of all trades* (Topic 12T159).

No. 30, on *The wide Midlands* (see above) and *Waterloo to Peterloo* (Argo Records ZFB68).

2. Other records which include industrial songs:
The collier's rant (Topic TOP74).
Along the coaly Tyne (Topic 12T189).
Oldham's burning sands (Topic 12TS206).
Tommy Armstrong of Tyneside (Topic 12T122).
Owdham Edge (Topic 12T204).
Canny Newcassel (Topic 12TS219).
Men at work (Topic TPS166).
Jack Elliott of Birtley: the songs and stories of a Durham miner (Leader LEA4001).
The Elliotts of Birtley: a musical portrait of a Durham mining family (Transatlantic Records XTRA1091).
The ballad of John Axon (Argo RG 474).
The big hewer (Argo RG 538).

Books

1. Song books (other than those mentioned in the list of sources):

A. L. Lloyd, *Come all ye bold miners*, Lawrence and Wishart, 1952; reprinted, 1974.

E. MacColl, *The shuttle and cage*, Workers' Music Association, 1954.

Roy Palmer, *A touch on the times*, Penguin, 1974.

Roy Palmer, *Songs of the Midlands*, E. P. Publishing, 1972.

M. Pollard, *Ballads and broadsides*, Pergamon, 1969.

G. and M. Polwarth, *North country songs*, Frank Graham, 1969.

2. The industrial revolution:

J. Addy, *A coal and iron community in the industrial revolution*, Longman, 1969.

P. Davies, *Children of the industrial revolution*, Wayland, 1972.

K. Dawson, *The industrial revolution*, Pan, 1972.

B. Inglis, *Poverty and the industrial revolution*, Hodder, 1971.

P. Lane, *The industrial revolution*, Batsford, 1972.

M. Rochester and B. J. Smith, *Children in industry* (folder), University of Keele, n.d.

E. P. Thompson, *The making of the English working class*, Gollancz, 1963.

B. Trinder, *The industrial revolution in Shropshire*, Phillimore, 1973.

3. Various trades:

R. Challinor, *The Lancashire and Cheshire Miners*, Frank Graham, 1972.

H. and B. Duckham, *Great pit disasters*, David and Charles, 1973.

W. Felkin, *History of machine wrought hosiery and lace manufacture*, 1867.

E. Peel, *Risings of the Luddites*, Heckmondwike, 1888 (reprinted Cass, 1968).

There is an excellent bibliography of books on coal mining in B. Lewis, *Coal mining*, Longman, 1971.

G. I. H. Lloyd, *The cutlery trades*, 1913.

M. Tomalin, *Coal mines and miners*, Methuen, 1960.

R. L. Galloway, *A history of coal mining in Great Britain*, 1882; reprinted David & Charles, 1972.

A. R. Griffin, *Coal mining*, Longman, 1971.

J. Dawes, *Coal mining*, Black, 1960.

Visits

There is a wealth of museums, sites and monuments connected with nineteenth century industry in this country. There are extensive lists of these in R. A. Buchanan's excellent book, *Industrial archaeology in Britain*, Penguin, 1972. See also B. Bracegirdle, *The archaeology of the industrial revolution*, Heinemann, 1973.

Local studies

Many local events – strikes, trade union activity, particular branches of industry, trades and crafts – have been very little studied. Local newspapers, factory archives, memoirs and autobiographies, Record Office materials – such are some of the possible sources, as well as visits to sites and museums. In all this, the living witness of men and women should not be forgotten.

Sources

Songs

1. Text: abridged from *Miscellaneous songs relating to Sheffield* (in J. Wilson, *The songs of Joseph Mather*, Sheffield, 1862), p.88. The tune indicated is *Cease, rude Boreas*, and the version of this which has been used is from Cecil Sharp MS No. 2128 by permission of the Cecil Sharp Estate.

2. Text: F. Peel, *The risings of the Luddites*, 1888, p.120. Tune: from a traditional source, via the singing of Bill Price on the record, *The fine old Yorkshire gentleman* (FHR038).

3. Text abridged from a broadside without imprint in the Kidson Collection, Mitchell Library, Glasgow. Tune: *The labouring man*, collected by Lucy Broadwood (*Journal of the Folk Song Society*, 1, p.198, published by the English Folk Song and Dance Society).

4. Text: two fragments collected by Rowland Kellett (*English Dance and Song*, Autumn 1969, p.93). Verse 1 originally had the title, *An owers is t'mill*, and verse 2, *T'mill a'll go*. I have put the two fragments together, very lightly adapted them, and set them to a variant of *The seven joys of Mary*, a tune which was sometimes used for songs of a social or political character.

5. Text: the same source as No. 4. The tune which would appear to be indicated by the metre is *Castles in the air*.

6. Sung by Tom Daniel, Batley, Yorks.; collected by A. E. Green, 1965; published by permission of A. E. Green and the Director of the Institute of Folk Life Studies, University of Leeds. (Previously published in A. L. Lloyd, *Folk song in England*, Lawrence and Wishart, 1967, p.328.)

7. As sung by the Irish Country Four on their Topic Record, *Songs, ballads and instrumental tunes from Ulster*, 12TS209, 1971.

8. Text: broadside printed by Harkness of Preston (Madden Collection, Cambridge University Library). Tune (not specified): *The brisk young lively lad*, collected by Lucy Broadwood (*Journal of the Folk Song Society*, 1, p.60).

9. In R. A. Church, *Economic and social changes in a Midland town: Nottingham*, 1968 (published by Frank Cass & Co. Ltd) p.92. Tune: written by Tony Seymour of Belbroughton, Worcs.

10. Text: broadside probably printed by J. Bromley of Kidderminster. The original has apparently disappeared, but a typescript copy has been preserved in the Kidderminster Public Library, Tune (not specified): the first part of *The lass of Cumberland* (W. Chappell, *Popular music of the olden time*, 1859, p.504). Although the tune dates from the seventeenth century it is similar in feeling to some of the carol tunes which are known to have been used by unemployed workmen in the nineteenth century.

11. Text (slightly abridged): broadside printed by Harkness of Preston (Madden Collection, 18/1231). The tune which would appear to be indicated by the metre is *A-nutting we will go*, in a version from Frank Kidson's *Traditional tunes*, 1891, p.163.

12. Text (abridged and adapted): J. Gutteridge, *Lights and shadows in the life of an artisan*, 1893, p.153. The original text was a parody of Tom Hood's poem, *The pauper*. If this was set to music, I have not been able to discover the tune. I have used that of a cockfighting song collected by Cecil Sharp, by permission of the Cecil Sharp Estate.

13. From the singing of Mr Wesley Perrins, of Stourbridge, Worcestershire, collected by Pamela Bishop.

14. Text: M. H. W. Fletcher, *Netherton: Edward I to Edward VIII*, Dudley Public Libraries, 1969, p.17 (originally published in 1946). Mr Fletcher dates the song at 1852, but gives no source. Tune: written by Pamela Bishop, formerly of Birmingham.

15. Text: J. Wilson Jones, *A history of the Black Country*, Cornish Brothers, Birmingham n.d., p.111. Tune (not indicated): *Tramps and hawkers*.

16. Text: under the title of *The grinders, or the saddle on the right horse*, in A. L. Lloyd, *Folk song in England*, 1967, p.364. *Tally i o, the grinder* is a comic song about marital incompatibility, and its tune was obviously intended for our song. I have been unable to trace it, however, and I have used a version of the poaching song, *Thorney Moor Woods*, which has a similar metre (collected by E. J. Moeran, *Journal of the Folk Song Society*, 7, p.14; adapted).

17. Text (adapted): broadside without imprint in the Kidson Collection, 'Written by Sextus Adams, author of some of the most popular comic songs, and duets, sung by the Principal Artistes in the Profession. Sung by Will Elair, with Great applause... Music... can be had from the author or 14 stamps, 25, Garibaldi-st., Everton, Liverpool'. The song is clearly based on *Jim the carter lad*, and I have used a version of the tune collected by Peter Kennedy, Folktracks and Soundpost Publications, Centre for Oral Traditions, Totnes, Devon.

18. Sung by Mr Samuel Webber of Birmingham (born in Poplar in 1874); collected by Roy Palmer, 16 July 1971.

19. Sung by Mr Joe Mallen of Kinver, Worcestershire (born 1891); collected by Roy Palmer, 24 April 1972; slightly adapted. The same song, with two verses fewer, was collected from Mr Mallen by Elizabeth Thomson in 1959 and published in *Songs of the Midlands* (ed. Roy Palmer, E. P. Publishing, Wakefield, 1972).

20. Text: Walter Haydn Davies, *The right place, the right time*, Llyfrau'r Dryw, Llandybie, 1972, p.90. Tune: *Lili Lon*.

21. Text: as No. 20, p.122. Tune: *Looking this way*.

22. Sung by Mr William Hill of Castleford, Yorkshire; collected by A. E. Green, 1966. (Previously published in A. L. Lloyd, *Folk song in England*, s.n.: *I am a driver*).

23. Text: broadside printed by Harkness of Preston (Madden Collection). Tune (not specified): *Hannah McKay* (Sam Henry Collection, Belfast Public Library).

24. Text: broadside printed by Wrighton of Birmingham (Firth Collection, Sheffield University Library). Wrighton was in business from about 1810 until 1830. Tune (not specified): *Castleroe Mill* (Sam Henry Collection).

25. Text (abridged): broadside printed by Such of London, under the title of *The miner's song, or, Five in the morning* (Firth Collection). Pearson of Manchester issued an almost identical text. Tune (not specified): *The carter's song*, collected by Lucy Broadwood (*Journal of the Folk Song Society*, 5, p.271); adapted.

26. Text: broadside printed by Pearson of Manchester, under the title of *The collier lads who labour under ground*, (Q 398.8 S.9, vol. 2, p.378, Manchester Central Library). A very similar text was issued by Pratt of Birmingham, who was printing from about 1840 until 1860. The song seems to be based on *We shepherds are the best of men*, and I have used a version of this tune, as sung by Fred Jordan of Shropshire.

27. Text (abridged): broadside printed by Pearson of Manchester (Firth Collection), under the title of *The miners' song. Down amongst the coals*. Tune (not specified): *Down in a coal mine* (A. L. Lloyd, *Come all ye bold miners*, Lawrence and Wishart, 1952, p.125).

28. Text: broadside without imprint, entitled *The lover's lament for John Sneddon. A collier* (Firth Collection). Tune: *A collier lad* (Sam Henry Collection).

29. Sung by Mrs A. Cosgrove, Newtongrange, Midlothian; collected by Peter Kennedy, Folktracks and Soundpost Publications, (as above No. 17).

30. Text (slightly adapted): sung by a man breaking stones on the road between Tipton, Staffordshire, and Dudley, Worcestershire, about 1850; given in an article by W.

H. Duignan, 'The Dudley riots', in the *Dudley Post*, January 1881. The song is identical in metre with *The Shropshire militia boys,* and a version of this tune has been used. In fact, it is the only version of the tune ever recorded. I have it from Jon Raven, who obtained it from John Evans of Caer Gwrie, Flintshire, who learned it from Wilf Darlington of Oswestry, who got it from the singing of his grandmother in 1968. A different version of the song was published in 1972, with a tune by Pamela Bishop (in *Songs of the Midlands)*.

31. Text: Walter Haydn Davies, *The right place, the right time*, p.71. English translation by Wyn Francis. Tune: *Ffarwel i blwy Llangywer (Farewell to old Llangower)*.
32. Text: broadside printed by Pratt of Birmingham (Firth Collection). Tune (not specified): *The masons* (Greig MSS, Aberdeen University Library).

Prose extracts

T. S. Ashton and J. Sykes, *The coal industry of the eighteenth century*, 1929; reprinted Manchester University Press, 1964.
J. Brown, *A memoir of Robert Blincoe*, Manchester, 1832.
Elihu Burritt, *Walks in the Black Country*, 1869.
Thomas Burt, *Autobiography*, T. Fisher and Unwin, 1924.
V. L. Davies and H. Hyde, *Dudley and the Black Country, 1760-1860*, Dudley Public Libraries, 1970.
Walter Haydn Davies, *The right place, the right time*, Llyfrau'r Dryw, Llandybie, 1972.
William Dodd, *The factory system illustrated*, 1844.
First report of the commission on the employment of children, 1842.
J. Gutteridge, *Lights and shadows in the life of an artisan*, 1893.
C. Hardwick, *History of the borough of Preston*, 1857.
W. Hutton, *Life*, 1816.
J. Wilson Jones, *The history of the Black Country*, Cornish, Birmingham, n.d.
The King of the Norfolk Poachers, *I walked by night*, ed. L. R. Haggard, Collins, 1939.
R. E. Leader, *Reminiscences of old Sheffield*, Sheffield, 1876.
Notes and Queries for Bromsgrove, vols. 1 and 2, Bromsgrove, 1909, and vol. 4, Bromsgrove, 1914.
L. Simonin, *Mines and miners*, 1868.
M. Walton, *Sheffield, its story and its achievements*, 4th ed., S. R. Publishers and the Corporation of Sheffield, 1968.
Thomas Wilson, *The pitman's pay*, (poem), Gateshead, 1830.

Illustrations

Pages 1 and 40 from L. Simonin, *Mines and Miners* 1868 photograph Cambridge University Library; pp. 6, 8, 13, 15, 16, 17, 23, 25, 26, 31, 32, 33, 38, 46, 49, 51(bottom), 61, Mansell Collection; p.37 Clifford Willetts; p.41 from T. H. Walton *Coal Mining* 1885, photograph Birmingham University Library; pp.42, 45 from *First Report to the Commissioners on the Employment of Children* 1842, photographs by Cambridge University Library; p.51 Bill Pardoe; p.10 Tolson Memorial Museum; p.35 Radio Times Hulton Picture Library; pp.54, 55, 56 Central Press Agency; back cover Trades Union Congress.

Index of Songs

First lines are shown in italic

All you that love a bit of fun 19
At five in the morning 48
Attend awhile, you workmen 50
The brave Dudley boys 58
Brother workmen, cease your labour 7
The carpet weavers' true tale 21
The collier 46
The collier lads 50
The collier lad's lament 60
The collier lass 44
Come all you croppers 9
Come all you pretty fair maids 53
The Coventry weaver 24
The day was dark 21
The doffing mistress 18
Down among the coal 52
Down the pit we want to go 39
The factory bell 11
Five in the morning 48
Foster's Mill 9
From morn till night 29
The Gresford disaster 56
The handsome factory girl 19
Holly ho 36
I am a driver 41
I'll sing you a song 36
I'm a collier, it's true 46
In taking of my lonely walk 60
Joe, the factory lad 34
The jovial cutlers 7
The knocker up 13
Lament for John Sneddon 53
The matchgirls' song 35
The merry shoots 20
The morn is black 12
My name is Joe 34
My name's Polly Parker 44
The nailmakers' strike 27
Nailers' song 26
O bury the blackleg 59
O bury now the blackleg 59
Oh do you know her or do you not 18
Oh happy man, oh happy thou 11
'Ommer, 'ommer, 'ommer 26
A pal of mine once said to me 13
The pony driver 41
The poor nailmaker 29
Poverty knock 14
Poverty, poverty knock 14
The Preston steam-loom weaver 22
The Sheffield grinder's a terrible blade 30
Tally i o, the grinder! 30
Times they bin mighty queer 58
We'll hang old Bryant 35
Who is that man coming up the street 24
With rum and gin and brandy O 20
Working today 39
You men of wealth and luxury 52
You nailmakers all 27
You power-loom weavers far and near 22
You've heard of the Gresford disaster 56